JAY A. COHEN

Cloud Computing for Every Business
Getting the Most Out of Your Technology Spending

Jay A. Cohen

Copyright © 2019

All Rights Reserved

ISBN: 9781702162227

Dedication

This book is dedicated to all the businesses out there that have been badly and incorrectly educated on cloud technology. Small businesses cannot afford an expensive Chief Information Officer or Vice President of Information Technology. It is my hope that this is the start of the readers' journey towards understanding the cloud and how it can work for their companies.

It will not give you the skills to do it yourself, but you will be able to speak more confidently to your contracts and consultants thanks to it. Whether you decide to use some of the cloud's tools to augment your infrastructure or you are ready to implement your whole "all in" strategy, make sure you are working with the consultants with the correct skill sets.

Acknowledgment

Since this was my first book, I knew it would take a lot of time. I also knew I needed to look for mentors to help guide and advise me. Luckily, I was able to work with some amazing mentors who could help with this. As such, I want to acknowledge them here. Thank you to my team of researchers and editors and authors in their own right. I will forever be grateful to them.

In addition, I want to thank my clients, past, current, and future, who fill me with the experiences and stories that I take with me to every new solution.

JAY A. COHEN

About the Author

Jay A. Cohen is the founder and CEO of JAYCO Cloud Computing Solution. With over 25 years of customer service and information technology experience, Mr. Cohen has worked with companies changing the face of the Information Technology industry. Aside from helping emerging technologies and guiding new startups, Mr. Cohen has also served on the boards of several non-profits, helping them grow. Furthermore, Mr. Cohen is an accomplished speaker who has spoken to countless groups on technology and the motivation in the workforce.

Preface

In today's modern world, technology is vital to every business. With its advance taking over every aspect of our life, there comes uncertainty of how we should navigate the plethora of new and emerging technologies. Who do you hire? What do they need to know? And how can you invest in your company without spending a fortune and without wasting what you are already spending?

Hiring the right person, team, or consultants can be very daunting to the non-technical manager. Questions like, *"Why do you think you need this?"* can throw any uncertain manager into a fright. Make no mistake, cloud computing is here, and it is not going away anytime soon. The ability to use a "pay-as-you-go" subscription model is more flexible and agile than budgeting as a capital expense, waiting for that budget to be approved, and then waiting for the year to start.

No – for a company to stay on top of its game, it must stay on the edge of new technology, whether it be Blockchain, Machine Learning, or Artificial Intelligence (AI). It can also use virtual private clouds for your corporate environment. Having the ability to retain data and reduce the anxiety of hardware failures is where cloud will excel and your company will flourish.

After reading this book, you should be able to understand the basics of the cloud and which of the big providers can help you. Even the big three cloud providers have a list of consultants that can help you start your cloud experience – supporting any project, large or small. So, read on to learn more about this exciting new emerging field!

Contents

Dedication .... *i*
Acknowledgment .... *ii*
About the Author .... *iii*
Preface .... *iv*
Chapter 1 3
What Is Cloud Computing? 3
Chapter 2 30
History of Cloud Computing 30
Chapter 3 47
Big Guys vs. Small Guys 47
Chapter 4 63
Big Cloud Players 63
Chapter 5 79
Carbon Footprints 79
Chapter 6 95
Capital and Operating Expenses 95
Chapter 7 110
Total Cost of Ownership 110
Chapter 8 129
The Benefits of Cloud Computing 129
Chapter 9 149
Web Hosting vs. Cloud Hosting 149
Chapter 10 168
Making the Cloud Work for You 168
Bibliography 185
Contact the Author 186

JAY A. COHEN

"Cloud computing services can be turned on or off quickly as needed, just like water in your tap. There is a team of dedicated professionals making sure the service provided is safe, secure and available on a 24/7 basis. When the tap isn't on, you're saving water and you aren't paying for resources you don't currently need."

-Vivek Kundra, CIO in the Obama administration

Chapter 1
What Is Cloud Computing?

Cloud Computing is the delivery of on-demand computing services – from applications to storage and processing power – typically over the internet and on a pay as you go basis. It enables the user to manage, process and store data remotely. This service is typically used through a server in a data center or a personal computer. A company buys access to storage from cloud service providers, as well as via access to applications

Owning one's own Information Technology (IT) infrastructure can be difficult and expensive to maintain. It is a far better option to pay for what one uses only when one has to use it. The best part is that you can pay on a monthly subscription basis rather than having to pay a large upfront capital expense. By utilizing the cloud companies that use cloud computing services, firms can benefit from economies of scale by taking advantage of the huge buying power and the cost savings associated with cloud computing.

Cloud Computing Characteristics and Benefits

Trading Capital Expense (CapEx) for Operating Expense (OpEx)

Instead of budgeting capital expenditures and investing heavily in servers, data centers, power, and cooling, without actually knowing how you're going to be using them, you can pay for the computing resources that you consume and only pay for how much you consume.

Benefit from Massive Economies of Scale

There are thousands of users utilizing the cloud, which helps providers benefit from economies of scale, which ultimately leads to lower-as-you-go prices. This means that by using cloud computing, you actually have to pay less than what you would have paid on your own.

Stop Guessing Capacity

Whilst creating an application, you might have to worry about the infrastructural capacity needs and make a decision about setting up the capacity. This can lead to either having too many idle resources at hand or having limited capacity. However, with cloud computing, this problem goes away since you can use only what is required as you scale up and down.

Increase Speed and Agility

Development happens at a fast pace when using cloud computing to support developers. When using cloud computing, IT resources are only a click away – resources which would have otherwise taken weeks to deliver. This increases the agility for the organization by decreasing the cost and time needed to experiment on projects and to develop them.

Stop Spending Money on Running and Maintaining Data Centers

The time you would have spent on stacking, racking, and powering servers can now be spent on your customers. With cloud computing, you can focus on projects that will help differentiate your business rather than your infrastructure.

Go Global in Minutes

Cloud computing allows you to launch your application in multiple regions of the world within a matter of a few seconds. This means that you can provide your customers with lower latency a better experience and charge them the minimal cost to access your application.

Cloud Computing Can Save Companies' a Majority of their IT Related Expenses

Cloud computing is a fast-growing industry. It allows users to access their data from anywhere via the internet. However, there have been apprehensions on the part of users around security, reliability, getting businesses, and understanding how they can use this as a hybrid to their own enterprise. Today, Amazon Web Services (AWS) has over 5000 Government agencies, 3000 Educational and Non-profit organizations, and over 17500 Businesses availing its services. In addition to AWS, there are many others that use a hybrid of cloud services, such as Microsoft Azure and Google Cloud, as well as a few other smaller providers.

Companies with sprawling infrastructures have the money and budgets to support large costs. They are mainly just concerned about a lack of control over the servers and security while using cloud computing. However, companies with pre-established computing capabilities should also look into this option and not dismiss it outright. Hybrid cloud computing offers huge financial and operational benefits, with spending on technology infrastructure kept at a minimal. Costs will drop in the following areas:

Lower Hardware Procurement Cost

Capital expenses can be reduced because instead of paying for in-house hardware equipment and operating systems, you could save up on this expense. Cloud computing usually has no licensing fee with a few exceptions – for example, Microsoft products come at a cost, but it has a lower monthly cost.

Cloud vendors update the software regularly. Businesses

can rest assured that they will have the most recent version of the software installed and that they will not have to incur any of the cost involved in upgrading the software or infrastructure.

Higher Speed

The traditional on-site operating system can take up to two years depending on budget cycles and manufacturing and shipping times. Whereas the Operating Expenses (OpEx) model can reduce that to just acquiring it, and that is it.

Reduced Maintenance and Labor Cost

With cloud solutions, companies have to pay less in the way of labor, support, maintenance, and operating costs. There is no need for a large, in-house IT department since all the equipment and hardware is managed by cloud computing vendors. This will enable an IT department to focus on other IT essentials that will help improve overall efficiency.

The IT costs saved will be on power and cooling, and floor space will be in square footage. With cloud and virtual servers, instead of needing one administer per server or 1 in 5 servers, you can now have one person overseeing 100 servers. Also, with the shared responsibility model, the cloud provider does the backend of overseeing the servers so that each company has less to worry.

Improved Reliability

Cloud solutions store their client's data on highly secure data centers. They are hosted on encrypted servers and their set up with redundancy is what makes them more reliable than in-house storage facilities. Amazon recently added a new redundancy service to their S3 data storage service. Amazon now claims that the data stored in the "durable storage" class is 99.9% "durable."

Their IT technicians are highly skilled and efficient, and reliably take care of encryptions and firewalls, as well as resolving all hardware issues. These costs may add up over time in traditional computing infrastructure. Therefore, it is far better to invest in cloud computing instead, as it is more efficient.

Reduced Operational Cost

The dependency on a large workforce is not required anymore. Cloud providers are the ones who will manage all software, servers, and hardware. This means that organizations can now focus on improving their operations and efficiencies. The money that they save in the process can be reinvested in the requirements of their core business objectives. For companies that want to utilize new software without heavy investment in technology, cloud solutions might be the best possible option. Nevertheless, you can more accurately "right-size" your servers. There is no need to overspend on a server that is barely used, and you don't want to spend too little on a server that is underpowered. With cloud computing, you can increase or decrease the size of your storage and computing power, so you only need to pay for what you use. Cloud providers can manage servers and software (servers are hardware, so kind of redundant) and few IT staff are required to manage servers when they are virtual.

Improved Productivity

Instead of learning, supporting, and maintaining software themselves, companies can now focus on their core business objectives. Adopting cloud software allows companies to use well-organized processes and workflows. It can take physical computer systems months to become fully operational because of budgeting processes, manufacturers' delivery schedule, and set up to organizational specifications and burn-in, whereas it takes cloud computing only a matter of minutes. This is due to the fact that the software and hardware infrastructure of cloud solutions is already established. The way cloud solutions are designed automatically makes it easier for users to access them from anywhere in the world. This is known as Bring Your Own Device (BYOD), where all a user needs to ensure is that they have an internet device (such as a laptop, tablet, smartphone, etc.) and an internet connection. It is also designed in a way that allows businesses and professionals to use it on multiple devices. It is not static, unlike some of the conventional programs such as excel. This means workers can be as productive out of office hours as they would be during them.

Eliminates Capital Cost

Cloud vendors operate on a subscription, pay as you go, or usage-based pricing structures, meaning businesses will only ever pay for what they need. With traditional options, enterprises need to purchase an entire system, which includes spacing out the servers for a projected need that they may or may not have metrics for. This can result in over purchasing a server by buying something that is too large, or worse, under projecting and buying a server too small, regardless of whether they want to use its total functionality or not. Servers are not like traditional laptops and come with an operating system only. You might have to pay for the operating system depending on the manufacturer. Companies either require you to purchase software off the shelf or create their own. Some of the software products, like SharePoint by Microsoft, can cost up to $25,000 or more for a year's use. Alternatively, you can make monthly payments for it as a cloud user.

However, with cloud computing, upfront costs are lower since they only have to pay for the package required, nor are there any license fees. The investment costs for a traditional approach are quite high because they need to have their own internal hardware, servers, and equipment; all of which must be paid for upfront. Therefore, companies that want to use powerful software with low capital risk should opt for cloud solutions. In today's modern world, businesses depend on technology for innovation and accelerating growth. Cloud computing is not restricted to a physical storage device, so by adopting cloud computing enterprises, you will be able to improve productivity, develop new services, enter new markets, attract new customers, and improve operational efficiency. This will help the company stay one step ahead of the competition and speed up technological advancement – or at least not get left behind.

History of Cloud Computing

The term "cloud computing" started being used extensively in 2006 by large companies such as Google and Amazon. They meant the term "cloud computing" to describe the trend of people using computer software to save their files over the internet rather than on their desktops.

However, *Technology Review* tracked back to when the term was coined. This happened inside the office of Compaq Computer, where a group of technology executives was shaping the future of the internet. They called it "cloud computing." Thus, cloud computing was identified for the first time in 1996 by Compaq.

Like "Web 2.0," cloud computing has become a ubiquitous piece of jargon that many tech executives find annoying, but also hard to avoid. *"I hated it, but I finally gave in,"* says Carl Bass, President, and CEO of Autodesk, whose company unveiled a cloud computing marketing campaign in September 2011. He added, *"I didn't think the term helped explain anything to people who didn't already know what it is."*

Accessibility of Cloud Computing

Cloud can be accessed from anywhere as long as you have an internet connection. However, there is a latency problem. If the data is coming from another part of the world, it may be sluggish compared to a local connection. Latency problems even take place when the data is coming from the other side of a congested network.

There is another issue: data sovereignty. Many companies

in Europe are worried about their data being stored in centers in the United States. This would make this data available to US law enforcement agencies. This is the reason why big cloud vendors have built various regional data centers so organizations can keep their data in their own respective regions under their laws. In Germany, Microsoft has gone a step further and offered its Azure cloud services from two data centers. These have been set up to prevent the US authorities from having any access to customer data stored here. These data centers are under the control of a German company that acts as a "data trustee." Even Microsoft cannot access data at the sites without the permission of this German company. All this demonstrates that there is a demand to keep specific data in specific locations.

Regulations of cloud computing vary widely based on where it is located. For example, in China, there are strict technological regulations for this sector. This is why Amazon Web Services (AWS) has opened a second center in China; in the Ningxia Region that is operated by the Ningxia Western Cloud Technology.

The UK government has placed a lot of stress on its citizens and businesses to consider the country of origin of the vendors of cloud services that they might be using. There are some cybersecurity issues and antivirus software issues that need to be addressed while using cloud computing. Furthermore, there is an extreme threat of "digital fragmentation." This is a result of multiple countries enacting legislation that protect the privacy of the customers and enhance cybersecurity.

AWS GovCloud (US)

AWS GovCloud (US) is Amazon's cloud region designed to host sensitive data, regulated workloads, and address the most stringent U.S. government security and compliance requirements. In order to gain access to this region, you must have a root account holder or a vetted U.S entity.

This region is operated by employees that are U.S citizens on U.S soil. AWS GovCloud gives their partners, who happen to be vetted government agencies, the opportunity to create a cloud solution that is in accordance with Cloud Computing Security Requirements Guide (SRG) for Impact Levels 2, 4 and 5, FIPS 140-2, IRS-1075, Department of Defense (DoD), Export Administration Regulations (EAR), U.S. International Traffic in Arms Regulations (ITAR), the DOJ's Criminal Justice Information Systems (CJIS) and the FedRAMP High baseline. While using GovCloud, there are a lot of compliances that need to be addressed by customers at every stage of their cloud journey – be it export-controlled data to other forms of CUI, financial data to law enforcement data, and sensitive patient medical records to Personally Identifiable Information (PII).

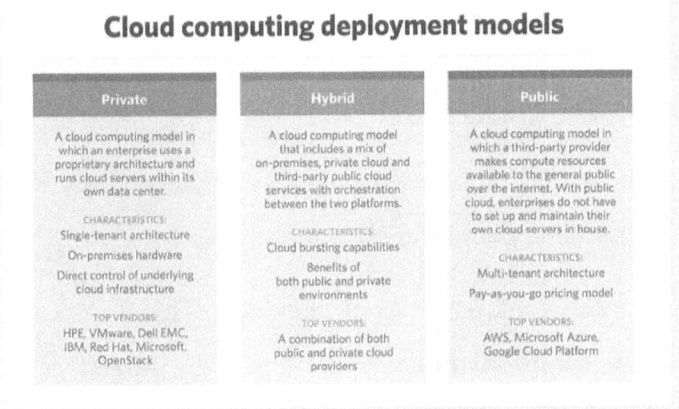

What is Public Cloud?

A public cloud is when a service provider makes resources, such as virtual machines, storage facilities, or applications, available to the general public over the internet. This offer can either be free of cost or can be offered with a pay-per-usage model.

Public Cloud Architecture

The public cloud has an environment that is fully virtualized. It has a basic architecture that all the tenants can use. This allows them to share computing resources. Even when this data is on the public cloud, it is nevertheless isolated from other tenants. In order to transmit data rapidly, it works on high-bandwidth network connectivity. The storage available in most cases is purposely provisioned and uses multiple data centers. It carefully duplicates all file versions. These characteristics are responsible for it gaining a reputation of flexibility.

Public cloud architecture can be further categorized by service models. Common ones include:

- **SaaS (software as a service):** This is a software distribution model in which a third-party provider hosts application and makes them available to customers over the internet. It is the delivery of applications as a service. This is a version of cloud computing that people are most used to. In this case, the underlying operating system and hardware are of no use to the end-user. This service can be accessed via a browser or an app. It is usually bought on a per-user basis. For example, Salesforce, NetSuite, Concur, iCloud, Google Apps, Workday, Citrix, GoToMeeting, and WebEx.

- **PaaS (platform as a service):** This is a model in which a third-party provider hosts application development platforms and tools on its own infrastructure and makes them available to the customers over the internet. It provides the tools that applications are built on, which includes the developmental tool, operating system, database management, and middleware. It also includes an underlying virtual server. Good examples in this regard are; Google App Engine, Red Hat's OpenShift, and Heroku.

- **IaaS (infrastructure as a service):** This is a model in which a third-party provider hosts servers, storage, and other virtualized computer resources and makes them available to customers over the internet. It is a fundamental building block of computing that can be rented and exists in the form of networking, storage, and virtual servers. This is suited for companies that want to build applications from the very beginning and want to focus on other elements of their operations. Moreover, this requires them to match a certain skill level to navigate and organize the software. The top three providers for this are AWS, Microsoft Azure, and Google Cloud.

Public clouds are used mainly by private individuals who do not need the features of a private cloud, such as a high level of infrastructure or security. Organizations can still use it for its services like webmail, online document collaboration and non-sensitive content. The most popular examples are all encompassed by cloud computing and are publicly available. These include the following:

- Enterprise Management
- Development environments
- Online software application
- Storage devices
- Server hosting

Features and Benefits

Ultimate Scalability And Flexibility: There are fluctuations in activity during a certain period and to cater to these vital cloud resources, public cloud resources are available on-demand from the cloud's vast resources. Consider how a small company may only need one small server, but during peak times of use (let's say they announce a new product), the traffic to the website may be so great that even with high CPU usage capacity, it might not be enough to handle it.

Certain alerts are set so that more servers will be automatically spun up with load balancing to make sure each user is well served with no slowdown or outage. For every three seconds of page load time, you lose a client forever.

Then, when the traffic is lower, it automatically spins down a server that is no longer needed. For flexibility, consider if clients notice more traffic all the time instead of spinning up and down servers as most of the time, they may need a bigger server. With flexibility, the client can opt for a larger server, and they can be moved to a large server without ever taking them down. We simply add or subtract CPUs or Memory or Storage to that end.

Utility Style Costs: As public clouds offer a pay-as-you-go billing model, consumers only have to pay for what they use, when they use it, and obtain exactly the resources they need.

Cost-Effective: Where the companies are benefiting because of the vast resources available on public clouds, but the credit really goes to no capital cost, no budget review, and no planning for capital spending. The cloud providers have incredible buying power because they buy on such a large scale that they can get servers and disk space at such a low cost that they can pass those savings on to the end-user, undercutting the resources of the operations.

Reliability: The reliability is high because of the redundancy configurations. There are a number of servers and networks involved in creating a public cloud, so even if one component fails, others will not be affected and the services will continue to run efficiently. Some cloud providers, such as Amazon S3, are designed to provide 99.999999999% durability and 99.99% availability of objects over a given year.

Location Independence: The public cloud can be accessed from anywhere with an internet connection. This makes it easier for clients to work from anywhere at any time. It's basically a means of increasing productivity without losing a lot of precious time. For example, even when natural disasters strike, employees can go wherever they have power and an internet connection and your operations will not be disrupted.

Table 1. Worldwide Public Cloud Services Forecast (Millions of Dollars)

	2016	2017	2018	2019	2020
Cloud Business Process Services (BPaaS)	40,812	43,772	47,556	51,652	56,176
Cloud Application Infrastructure Services (PaaS)	7,169	8,851	10,616	12,580	14,798
Cloud Application Services (SaaS)	38,567	46,331	55,143	64,870	75,734
Cloud Management and Security Services	7,150	8,768	10,427	12,159	14,004
Cloud System Infrastructure Services (IaaS)	25,290	34,603	45,559	57,897	71,552
Cloud Advertising	90,257	104,516	118,520	133,566	151,091
Total Market	209,244	246,841	287,820	332,723	383,355

Source: Gartner (February 2017)

- Users can now successfully use the most capable public cloud IaaS for new, as well as existing

applications. This enables the efficiency of both, infrastructure and developer productivity to increase by a great margin.
- The market has now split into providers with hyperscale IaaS+PaaS. People who want to become such providers, niche-oriented providers with specialized capabilities, and providers accommodating "rented virtualization" can now take advantage of cloud optimization.

What Is A Private Cloud?

The private cloud is a secure model of cloud computing in which only specified clients operate. It provides computing power as a service within a virtual environment with an underlying computing resource. The model is only accessible to a single organization so that it enjoys greater control over and privacy of its data.

You can even have a private cloud which is not on-premises. Virtual Private Cloud (VPC) is an on-demand configurable pool of shared computing resources allocated within a public cloud environment that helps in providing a certain level of isolation between different organizations using the resources. Virtual Private Clouds are commonly used with Infrastructure as a Service (IaaS) providers. This isolation of one particular VPC user from all the others (VPC and other public cloud users) and working with infrastructure as a structure is achieved by allocating this VPC user with a private IP subnet and virtual communication construct – for example, a VLAN.

The VPC provides isolation within a cloud and is secured through authentication and encryption to provide the organization access to its VPC cloud resources. By providing certain isolation levels, the organization can work on a "virtually private" cloud similar to their on-premise environment. Hence, you are essentially operating a private cloud within a public cloud.

A real-life example of how the VPC is implemented is when in August 2009, Amazon Web Services launched Amazon Virtual Private Cloud, which allows the Amazon Elastic Compute Cloud service to be connected to legacy infrastructure over an IPsec virtual private network connection. Having the same VPC and infrastructure provider can help improve the communication process and help cut down on any confusion between the user and the vendor. Virtual Private clouds create a more secure environment on public infrastructure.

Features and Benefits of Private Clouds

Higher Security And Privacy: Private cloud offers high security to organizations. This is achieved through access being restricted to connections made from on-site internal hosting, dedicated leased lines, and organizations' firewall.

More Control: They can create network solutions based on their own needs. It can be managed online, and configurations can be made by a single organization using the private cloud.

Cost And Energy Efficiency: The organization using a private cloud can benefit from it because it can improve the allocation of resources. The demands of various departments can be met through the functions being provided to each of them. It can help to reduce the carbon footprint of the organization and is more efficient than LANs.

Improved Reliability: The creation of a virtual operating environment means that the network can carry on working, even if it fails somewhere in the physical infrastructure. The resources can be pulled from the unaffected servers, even if they are all hosted internally.

Cloud Bursting: If a function of a private cloud requires space, it can achieve it from the public cloud by switching on that particular function. This usually happens when there is a rise in demand and is known as cloud bursting.

What Is A Hybrid Cloud?

A hybrid cloud is an integration of a private cloud and a public cloud. It performs distinct functions within a single organization. It can also be a public cloud with an on-premise location. Public cloud services are more cost-efficient and scalable than private cloud services. Therefore, a company can utilize public cloud services for all non-sensitive operations and private clouds for where they require them. They can use private clouds when there is a security concern and use public clouds when they need to be more cost-effective. For example, they can host their e-commerce website on a private cloud whereas host their brochure site in a public cloud. This is collectively called hybrid cloud hosting.

Another example can be that the Infrastructure as a Service (IaaS) can follow a hybrid model. This could be done by storing client data and financial business data in a private cloud and using the public cloud when collaborating jointly on a document where the clients can work, monitor progress, and include their feedback as needed.

Hybrid cloud model can be implemented in the following ways:

- An organization can sign up for both, a private cloud as well as a public cloud that is then integrated into the system.
- A private cloud and a public cloud team up and provide services as integrated.
- Individual cloud providers provide a single hybrid cloud as a full package.

Features and Benefits

Flexibility: The availability of both the secure resources and scalable cost-effective public resources makes it flexible. It can provide organizations with an opportunity to explore different operational systems.

Security: The hybrid cloud service allows for data to remain secure and helps in data handling and storage when required.

Cost-Effectiveness: The public cloud allows one to benefit from economies of scales. The hybrid cloud allows companies to keep their high-security functions on the private cloud and keep their operations secure while saving expenses by storing non-essential information on a public one.

Scalability: The public cloud aspect of hybrid clouds will offer scalability with fewer restrictions since the resources are gathered from a larger cloud infrastructure. It can reduce the demand for the private cloud by moving the non-sensitive functions to the public cloud.

References

What is cloud computing? - Definition from WhatIs.com. (n.d.). Retrieved from https://searchcloudcomputing.techtarget.com/definition/cloud-computing

Hendrie, R. (n.d.). How Cloud Computing Can Save Your Company Money. Retrieved from http://blog.innervision.co.uk/blog/how-cloud-computing-can-save-your-company-mone

Regalado, A. (2013, December 30). Who Coined 'Cloud Computing'? Retrieved from https://www.technologyreview.com/s/425970/who-coined-cloud-computing/

Ranger, S. (2018, April 03). What is cloud computing? Everything you need to know about the cloud, explained. Retrieved from https://www.zdnet.com/article/what-is-cloud-computing-everything-you-need-to-know-from-public-and-private-cloud-to-software-as-a

"Flying by the seat of the pants must have been a great experience for the magnificent men in the flying machines of days gone by, but no one would think of taking that risk with the lives of 500 passengers on a modern aircraft. The business managers of a modern enterprise should not have to take that risk either. We must develop standard cloud metrics and ROI models, so that they can have instruments to measure success."

-Dr. Chris Harding, Director for Interoperability and SOA at The Open Group

Chapter 2
History of Cloud Computing

Cloud computing is not a new piece of technology. It has been around for the past fifty years. This chapter will take you on a journey from the birth of cloud computing to its current state in our world.

What Did We Do in the 60s?

This was the time when we had computers as big as the room they were placed in. So obviously, it was a logistical challenge to provide one for each user. How could multiple users access data and information if they wanted to at the same time and from different locations? The solution to this problem sprang up when a computer scientist named John McCarthy presented and, later on, initiated a project which would utilize a "time-sharing" system. This time-sharing system would allow multiple users to have shared access to heaps of data. Fortunately, it meant that finally, users could use a single central computer for accessing data at the same time. This theory eventually led to the foundation of cloud computing.

Making time-sharing the premise for cloud computing, the Defense Advanced Research Projects Agency (DARPA) offered a $2 million fund for Project MAC to MIT in 1963. DARPA provided the funding with the stipulation that MIT would have to come up with the technology that would allow more than one user to use a computer simultaneously. Thus, the foundation of the primitive form of cloud computing was laid, which allowed no more than two or three users to access information from the same computer simultaneously. Shortly after this in 1969, a computer scientist and a psychologist named J.C.R Licklider wanted to ambitiously make his vision of interconnecting people all around the world come true. He eventually helped in developing a network called Advanced Research Projects Agency Network (ARPANET). This set the steppingstones for the most primitive form of internet that we know today.

He had a vision, which he called an "Intergalactic Computer Network" that will make it possible for the masses to access information and connect, regardless of where they are located on the globe. The Intergalactic Computer Network later came to be known as the internet, which became one of the pillars in further developing cloud computing.

Breakthroughs throughout the 70s-80s

By this time, time-sharing had enough attention and work going on to find a full practical solution. 1970 was the year when the first concepts of virtual machines came to surface. Since the 1950s, the concept of shared access had already been introduced, but it needed a sound operating system to boost it to the next level and build its complete infrastructure. So, in the early 1970s, IBM developed and released an operating system called "Virtual Machines" (VM). A VM is simply an operating system which acts like a real computer, enabling the user to have the same experience as they would have on dedicated hardware.

Platforms like Multics, early UNIX ports, and Cambridge CTSS provided breakthrough solutions to fully engaging and incorporating the whole time-sharing concept on mass levels. The VM operating system completely changed the structure of the word "virtualization" because now the possibility of having multiple computing environments to reside on a single physical environment was fast becoming reality. Later in 1982, to make it possible for the world to experience cheap and fast connections that would eventually enable cloud computing, the first Ethernet adapter card was released for the IBM PC. Fast-forwarding to 1989, the first public dialup Internet Service Provider was founded –

namely, Software Tool & Die.

The 90s: The Cloud is Official

The 1990s were the time when the world was on the precipice of literally entering into a new century, with promises of technological advancement that will change the course of history for good. This was a time when the telecommunications industry was flourishing and spreading its routes farther than anyone could have anticipated just a few years ago. By the early 1990s, telecommunications companies took a huge leap when they started offering network connections that were private.

This meant that it was a network that made it possible for more than one user to access data and shared information from the same physical infrastructure. This was later termed as Virtual Private Network (VPN). The incredible advancement in telecommunications and virtual connections named this age as the start of the "internet age." In 1991, the European Organization for Nuclear Research (CERN) made it possible for the public to avail the internet for general use. Shortly after that, between 1993 and 1994, early browsers, such as Netscape and Mosaic, were launched. This breakthrough led to the development of a series of startup websites, including world-renowned "eBay," which was known as AuctionWeb at that time when it was founded by a French-born Iranian American computer programmer, Pierre Omidyar, in 1995. It was around the same time when the now well-known billion-dollar cloud computing company, Amazon.com, Inc., was launched.

Since the internet was the main contributor towards rising shared access, it is why soon after being declared as the constituent of a new age, the word "cloud" collectively surfaced. It was first used by Professor Ramnath Chellapa of Emory University in 1997, where he described it as the *"computing paradigm, where the boundaries of computing will be determined by economic rationale, rather than technical limits alone."* Soon after that, a series of evolutions were witnessed in terms of cloud computing. This took place in four different ways:

- Grid Computing: This was designed to solve huge problems with parallel computing.
- SaaS: This was a sort of a network-based subscription platform to applications.
- Utility Computing: It provided computing resources to people as a metered service.
- Cloud Computing: Astounding services that provided IT resources access from anywhere.

The following year, a software providing company was founded by the name of VMware. VMware made it possible to have a guest operating system, which was linked to virtualized sets of hardware. Later the same year, a milestone in the computing world was achieved with the upgrade of the Walter Reed Army Medical Center to 100 megabits/sec Asynchronous Transfer Mode network, which enabled the accommodation of Virtual Local Area Networks.

Racing to 1999, the world witnessed the launch of Salesforce.com in March, which was a company specializing in providing software as a service (SaaS). In the same year, Napster was launched, which is the first platform to provide sharing of digital audio files through internet services. In the present day, you can now download, stream and share your favorite music and songs on Napster.

The Dot-Com Bubble in the 2000s

Entering into a new century, internet-based businesses became the center of attention for investors. This was the new way of pumping in money for quick profits and came to be known as dotcom, in correspondence to the ".com" domain used for doing business over the internet. The dot-com investments poured in like never before due to the overnight success of a few internet companies.

However, this meant that the investors were investing tons of money in startups which had no long-term planning, or even a basic business plan mapped out. This eventually led to what is known as the *"dot-com boom"* or the *"dot-com bubble."* The dot-com bubble burst in 1999, mainly because of investors ignoring basic business metrics. In their run to make *"quick money,"* they trusted businesses that were mostly built on brand awareness and marketing.

By 2000, the bubble had burst completely, followed by a "dot-com crash" which led to the failure of countless startups due to investors pulling the dough. Only 48% of the dot-com companies survived, among which Amazon was one of the few successful companies that benefited. Following the dot-com bubble burst, Amazon promised to take the world into a new era of cloud computing.

Amazon launched a development product called Amazon Web Service in 2002, which turned Amazon into the first major organization who modernized their data centers. What magic trick did AWS pull off for Amazon? In the simplest explanation, Amazon Web Service is a collection of web services or remote computing services that were amalgamated into a cloud computing platform on the internet, through which Amazon provided online services to external customers.

The highlight of these services includes the EC2 and Amazon S3. The EC2, also known as the Elastic Compute Cloud from Amazon, allowed people to virtually rent computers so that they could use their applications and programs. However, Amazon was not the only major company which survived the dotcom bubble. Google, a name that even a layman recognizes and knows how to efficiently use today, launched Google Docs services in the same year. It revolutionized the blogging system by allowing users to edit, transfer and even collectively upload documents online, all at the same time. This was the internet-based low-cost storage and computing services that brought users up and close to the experience of limitless document sharing and computing.

A New Era of Private and Hybrid Cloud Computing

Soon after Google's internet-based editing and document transferring services, the best brains in the world joined forces to find a way to upgrade processors in terms of speed, as well as their capacity to process the gigantic amounts of data sets. World-famous universities like MIT, University of Washington, University of Maryland, and Stanford University got together with IBM and Google to provide the funding for the research. This was the same year when the cloud was used to launch the video streaming service by none other than Netflix. In the year 2008, a paid open-source computer software was released, which was used to build private and hybrid cloud computing environments that are AWS compatible. The software was originally developed by the Eucalyptus Systems. The good year for cloud computing did not just end here; development continued with Nasa's OpenNebula, which is an open-source cloud computing and management platform dealing with tens of thousands of VM and heterogeneous distributed data pieces. In 2008, it became the first open-source software for providing hybrid and private clouds.

With the launch of smartphones, including Apple's iOS platform and Google's Android, the need for boosting cloud services was now more important than ever. The availability, as well as the freedom of sharing and storing personalized information, which contained images, videos, and audios, introduced the need of having a framework that supported storage and access to such data. In 2011, focusing on the storage of personalized data, Apple launched the iCloud. The public, by this time, needed to know the extraordinary services cloud computing could potentially offer them, so Microsoft took it upon themselves to market iCloud in the form of advertisements on televisions and other media platforms.

Cloud Computing Timeline

1950 – Coming up with the concept of time-sharing.

1963 – MIT is given a fund to develop a primitive form of cloud computing.

1969 – ARPANET is developed by J.C.R Licklider, as well as the concept of the internet.

1969 – UNIX is developed.

1970 – The concept of Virtual Machines (VM) comes to the surface for the first time.

1970 – ARPANET is transformed into the internet.

1982 – The first Ethernet adapter card is released for the IBM PC.

1989 – The first public dialup Internet Service Provider is founded – namely, Software Tool & Die.

1990 – The age of internet begins, and the Virtual Private Network (VPN) is launched.

1991 – CERN makes the internet available for general public use.

1993 – Mosaic and Netscape are launched.

1995 – eBay is launched by Pierre Omidyar.

1995 – Amazon.com, Inc. is launched by Jeff Bezos.

1997 – The first time the term "cloud computing" is used by Ramnath Chellapa of Emory University.

1999 – Salesforce.com is launched in March by Marc Benioff, Parker Harris, Dave Moellenhoff, and Frank Dominguez.

1999 – The first audio file sharing platform named Napster is launched.

2000 – The dot-com bubble bursts.

2002 – Amazon introduces the world to Amazon Web Service (AWS), a remote computing services platform.

2006 – Amazon launches Elastic Compute Cloud (EC2).

2008 – Google launches the Google app Engine.

2008 – Eucalyptus is launched to provide private and hybrid cloud computing services, which are AWS compatible.

2008 – Nasa's OpenNebula becomes the first open-source software for providing hybrid and private clouds.

2010 – Microsoft steps into the cloud computing marketing after launching Microsoft Azure.

2011 – Apple launches iCloud for the storage of personalized data.

2011 – IBM launches SmartCloud.

2013 – Google launches the Google Compute Engine

The Future of Cloud Computing

Unlike the ruse of the dot-com bubble, there is no way that the world can shift from cloud computing. Many experts did claim that the computing façade will subside soon enough, but given the central role IT is playing in boosting the online business environment, it is hard to move away from it unless a stronger candidate comes along. So, does cloud computing have a safe future? Both commercially and publicly? And what are the trends of cloud computing presently?

Numbers show that the future of cloud computing is heading towards dynamic growth. According to analysis, cloud computing generated an estimated revenue of about $46.4 billion in 2008, with over a quarter of companies utilizing cloud-based applications to expand and boost their market. By 2013, the revenue had climbed to $150 billion dollars. With these numbers, it will be hard to think that there will be another dot-com bubble anytime soon.

Cloud computing has bridged the gap between effectively

reciprocating the service or product to the consumer. It is now easier to communicate exactly what the business intends to do. Consumers have never been so connected with the business world as they are right now. The customers are now able to express themselves almost immediately through interactive platforms, which helps with pursuing immediate improvisation.

Cloud computing will play an extremely important role in shifting tomorrow's world towards digital infrastructure. All the things we see in today's sci-fi movies, like automated transportation, digitally controlled air traffic, artificial intelligence; all could be made possible with the help of cloud computing, which is a heaven for data storage and analysis. As we speak, innovators are working right now to explore the potential of cloud computing. Consider Huawei, which is working on introducing Industry Cloud, which will have an area-oriented concentration. Industry based clouds like Banking Cloud and Utility Cloud will foresee their particular set of activities to ensure maximum productivity and utilization. Using industry-based clouds would most importantly save industries the inventory and transportation costs that take away huge sums from the total cost.

Since the advent of smartphones, it has been an undeniable fact that slowly, Artificial Intelligence will be the solution to everything. Since phones are the largest platform for cloud computing, AI is gradually making its way into smartphones. We already know that cloud computing is the future, but what exactly contributes to its growth? We already discussed the external factors, but a considerable amount of this rising trajectory is also due to the adoption of private and hybrid cloud computing. Private cloud computing is a model of cloud computing that works on a secure cloud-based environment for specific clients so they can operate. This restricts access exclusively to a single organization. Since 2016, the numbers have risen from 63% to 77% in terms of adopting private cloud computing. VPC (Virtual Private Cloud) is also being used exclusively because it provides the usage of a third-party provider's infrastructure instead of using private clouds over internal infrastructure. Since organizations are focused over a private secure network, private cloud computing seems to be the promising option for leading industries and companies.

Following the utilization of private clouds, hybrid cloud computing is also gaining widespread popularity. Adoption rates soar to 71% year after year. Organizations are acquiring hybrid clouds mainly because it allows them onsite services, as well as third party and public cloud services – that too in a technically controlled environment. Also, it is more secure and provides easy access to new technology.

The leap in public and private cloud computing has created strong security barriers for organizations, especially for government-based operations. This technology will soon play an important part in digitalizing the world, and every small business will be eventually fighting to adopt and even improvise this technology for further growth.

The numbers do the talking for VMs. There is new evidence out every day that points towards the promising future of this technology. Case in point: OpenStack rose from 13% to 19% and VMware rose from 33% to 44%, both of which are incredibly overwhelming. Nobody loses in this game; cloud computing is immensely advantageous for everyone involved. Hence, it should come as no surprise that it will play an important role in our society's future.

JAY A. COHEN

"We believe we're moving out of the Ice Age, the Iron Age, the Industrial Age, the Information Age, to the participation age. You get on the Net and you do stuff. You IM (instant message), you blog, you take pictures, you publish, you podcast, you transact, you distance learn, you telemedicine. You are participating on the Internet, not just viewing stuff. We build the infrastructure that goes in the data center that facilitates the participation age. We build that big friggin' Webtone switch. It has security, directory, identity, privacy, storage, compute, the whole Web services stack."

-Scott McNealy, *Former CEO, Sun Microsystems*

Chapter 3
Big Guys vs. Small Guys

When we talk about the categorization of businesses based on size, we usually observe two kinds of businesses: large enterprises, and small companies. Apart from the nature of the business, there are several differences between small and large organizations. Big sharks like Amazon, Microsoft, and Google, as were discussed in the previous chapter, have endless resources available to them – resources that are either human resources, financial resources, or technological resources.

Based on the ease of access to these vital business assets, these organizations provide services to their clients. However, when these companies came into existence, they did not start as a multi-million dollar companies. They all started as small business enterprises and then slowly became one of the largest companies in the world.

When a business is small and in a growing phase, its processes and ways of providing services to its clients are significantly different from those of a large organization. This chapter will shed light on the importance of cloud computing for a small business enterprise and how a small business can take advantages of cloud computing solutions. I am sure that you are aware of what kind of business is known as a small business. However, let me give you a brief overview. Any organization that has five hundred or even smaller number of employees, it is known as a small business enterprise. In the United States of America, about 99.9 percent of businesses are small companies, and these are the businesses that are considered to be the backbone of the economy. Now, if these organizations move towards the utilization of cloud computing solutions, then the massive improvement that they will be able to achieve in their operations will be unmatchable.

When an organization is operating at a small scale, it is usually limited by finances which is why they require cheaper methods of meeting the objectives of their businesses. For any business to be successful, it is important for the enterprise to establish a good rapport with its clients and customers. Specifically, when an organization is in its growing stage, it is vital for its long-term survivability to be able to address the concerns of its consumers round the clock.

Today, only the use of cloud computing enables an organization to maintain constant and continuous communication with its clients. In addition to that, the software and technology that is used for various business activities keep on changing every day. Courtesy to the rapid annual advancements in the field of technology, a new and much more enhanced version of software becomes available daily, having even more efficient features.

For small businesses, it is quite disadvantageous to spend a significant amount of money on a certain technology, and only after benefiting from it for a little while, they learn that it has become obsolete due to a competitor's product. A much better tool becomes available in the market to fulfil the same task that specifically poses a threat to the small businesses.

In order to survive the never-ending competition in the market, these companies need to use the most effective and latest technological resources to satisfy the needs and requirements of their clients. With cloud computing, these companies do not need to spend money on buying expensive software. Now, today, there are numerous software programs available on the internet that utilize cloud computing systems. All the business has to do is buy the monthly or yearly subscription to them. In some cases, companies do not even have to subscribe to a plan or anything. They can only pay for the services that they acquire. This way, it does not become a long-term asset for the business, and these small businesses can easily shift towards a different software whenever they feel the need of doing so.

Apart from having the ease of shifting towards improved technology, the businesses will no longer have to bear the expensive costs of such software if they move towards cloud computing solutions. Take accounting software into consideration. Having a small business, a business owner would want to save as much money as they can from spending on the accounts management as it is merely a need for the business. Before the cloud computing solutions became available, companies had to buy expensive software to fulfill their accounting purposes. Fortunately, now, vendors like FreshBooks and Zoho are available on the internet that help maintain all financial records at the low cost of $10/month. This actually proves to be very beneficial for those individuals who have sole proprietorship businesses, or work as freelancers and need to complete tasks like expense tracking, simple reporting and invoicing. Apart from that, if we talk about the storage and management of data, businesses have fulfilled this purpose of the business in several ways.

Businesses use servers to store their large data and

information. However, having your own server is not something that every business can afford to do. Servers themselves are not only expensive in terms of their cost, but also require expenditure on their constant maintenance. Today, even though servers are small, they still need power and cooling, which is expensive.

Nonetheless, you can put a server under your desk, and some small companies do. But a server under your desk has one disk and no redundancy. Most hard drives on servers are set up with groups of hard drives grouped together to create one drive where the data is equally distributed on the hard drives so that even if one drive dies, you don't lose all the data. You will just have to swap the drive out with a new one. Regardless, you still don't have the resources of the cloud. Other than that, these servers require constant maintenance as they might overheat r start malfunctioning, which can result in a massive amount of data loss – something that every business wants to avoid. In order to ensure their absolute working, you will have to hire an IT team that can look after the servers. So, add to your expenses not only the repairs and maintenance costs, but the salaries and benefits of the IT team you will be hiring as well. If we talk about large companies, this might not be an issue for them as they have greater availability of resources and finances to manage their own data centers.

Apart from that, the bigger the business is, the greater the data and information they need to store. So, storing such great amount of information using cloud-computing solutions might prove to be a little inefficient for such organizations when they can easily manage to maintain their own data centers onsite with their servers securing all of their sensitive information. However, if we talk about small businesses, there could not have been better solutions to the data storage problem other than the cloud computing solutions.

Looking at the expenses that come with storing data on servers, it becomes clear that it is not at all affordable for small enterprises. Small businesses do not need to hire an employee or hire a team of employees to manage and update software, install servers, and maintain them. Either they are for emails or other data and also to run backup. The cloud computing solutions frees the business from all such expenses and worries. A small enterprise does not need to worry about maintaining the data or application if they utilize the services of cloud computing solutions as all of that will be taken care of by the end of the cloud vendor.

In addition to that, small enterprises are in a constant state of growth and development. Therefore, their need to store and manage data keeps on fluctuating and changing. Now, when it comes to servers, as the storage demand decreases, your servers can go to waste as for that period, you will not be using them to their fullest capacity. In other words, you would be paying for something that you are not benefiting from in any way. It can be crucial for a small enterprise to have an extra expense, so it is better for these businesses to move towards cloud computing for data storage purposes. You can simply increase the cloud's capacity if your storage demand rises. Similarly, if there is a need to cut down the storage needs, cloud computing provides the business flexibility to automatically update the system as per the needs and requirements of the business. Not only can the storage capacity be altered as per the business requirements, but also the exchange and transfer of the data can also be adjusted accordingly by the cloud vendor.

The best part about this is that it proves to be exceedingly cost-effective for the businesses as they pay the cloud vendors only for the services that they use. This way, the small enterprises do not have to worry about bringing constant changes in their production processes and can continue to work flawlessly. Specifically, in the case of small businesses, having this level of flexibility due to cloud computing makes it possible for them to gain an advantage in the market. They are not only able to compete with other small businesses in the market, but also large organization thanks to the use of cloud computing solutions.

Another benefit that small businesses can reap from using cloud computing services is the enhancement of their productivity. When a business is in its growing phase, it is essential for it to focus on its efficiency and productivity. They need to be able to provide services to their clients round the clock in order to gain an edge in the severe competition in the market.

Business owners and employees have the ability to work anytime, from any place, by using cloud computing. It not only enables the business to build a good rapport with its customers but also allows the employees of the company to work with much better coordination. Small businesses will see massive changes in their business processes if they incorporate cloud computing as it would allow a constant transfer and exchange of data and information.

It is true that in to maintain quality of services, sometimes workers need the opportunity of working from their home. Cloud computing makes it possible to work from anywhere the employees would like. The workers get a chance of working comfortably from their homes and manage to meet the deadlines for their projects with exceptional efficiency. Sometimes, an employee even wishes to work extra on a specific task but does not wish to spend those extra hours at the office premises. When a business uses cloud computing, it makes it possible for the employees to put in their extra efforts into a project based on their own feasibility. This way, small businesses are able to maintain their services' quality while simultaneously reducing the interruptions and delays that may occur during production due to the utilization of cloud computing services.

When you acquire the services of a cloud-computing vendor, you free yourself from feeling the need to have various different applications to facilitate your business processes. For example, every organization needs to have a specific company email through which the employees can maintain internal communication. Other than that, to formulate important business documents and presentations, a company needs a certain software and application to fill this purpose as well.

There are countless other operations that are involved in any kind of business. Therefore, it becomes a hassle for a company to install and manage various applications to fulfill these tasks. Now, using cloud computing technology,

Google provides a wide range of all of these applications under one roof. As was mentioned in the previous chapter, Google is one of the largest cloud computing service providers.

Google Docs gives you the ability to write up important organizational documents and forms, and make presentations that can be used in your meetings with employees and clients. Not only that, it also provides you with an opportunity to save your important files online. This way, even if something goes wrong with your computer, you still have it saved on your Google drives.

In addition to all of this, Google apps for business also includes emails that a business can use as their internal correspondence system. In addition, they can use Google Sites to create websites. Now, this is one of the most amazing things about cloud computing because it is extremely cost-effective for businesses. You only have to pay $5 per month for each individual using these applications on the business's account. This becomes very beneficial for the small enterprise that has a limited number of employees that would be using these software and applications. As you might know, back in the days, Microsoft office suite was the pioneer of all the applications used for business purposes. However, the companies used to pay hundreds of dollars to buy and have it installed in their systems.

Back then, it used to be available only in desktop versions, so the businesses were bound to buy the complete version. Now, even Microsoft has moved towards cloud computing, providing a cloud-based edition of these applications that is known as Office 365. To adopt the services of Office 365, businesses only need to pay for an annual subscription. Office 365 also contains an added feature of online video conferencing.

Now the employees will have a chance to work on group projects with greater efficiency as they will be able to have meetings through Skype and stay in continuous correspondence through instant messaging feature. There is also a mobile application available for Office365 that business owners and employees can benefit from as they will be able to work at any time and from any place without feeling the need of firing up their laptop. Several other cloud computing service providers are also available in the market that offer access to all of these applications at very low costs. Take for example InfoStreet, Inc., which charges businesses only $10 for each individual per month and provides an employee directory, calendar scheduling, CRM, email, file sharing, and conference calling.

Having discussed all of these benefits, it becomes quite clear how advantageous it can be, especially for small businesses to use cloud-computing services. A major issue that small enterprises go through is having compatible applications that align perfectly with the needs and requirements of their business. Most businesses end up paying to get certain applications customized as per their specifications. With use of cloud computing services, a business can even save money on that.

Cloud applications have a feature of Application Programming Interface (API) through which a business can easily integrate the desired applications. Other than that, business can save themselves from the hassle of storing the data on the computers. When a cloud computing service is used, all the data is saved on the cloud vendor's server, saving the business a lot of space on its own computer. The facility for storing data on another entity's server provides a business with a wide range of advantages.

The greater mobility that is provided by the way cloud computing systems work is undeniable. Consider an organization that provides services for establishing and maintaining websites for several clients. If this company uses its own servers to back up and update the data on the client's website, it can only achieve success in doing so as long as its servers are working fine. In case a server goes down, the websites of all of the clients will also go down unless there is another server backing up the client's website.

Even the large organization can only manage a limited number of data centers to provide support to the client's websites. Using cloud computing services, cloud vendors have a network of servers that are always backing up the data. So, even if one of the cloud vendor's server crashes, another server will immediately move to provide support to the website. All of this happens so fast that no time lag is felt.

Other than that, the transfer and exchange of online data is only fast enough if the server upon which the website is dependent is located near the location of the user of the website. For the businesses who have customers situated in different countries and continents, data will take a lot of time to transfer from one server to another until it finally reaches the user.

As cloud computing is a complete network of servers placed in different parts of the world, a business can simply take advantage of the utilization of a server near its potential customers. This way, the customers do not feel any delay in the exchange of information, which makes it possible for the companies to ensure a better customer experience. Considering the fact that businesses no longer have to buy physical servers, cloud computing provides greater opportunities for small businesses to expand and enter new markets. Small businesses and large companies mostly have one difference which separates them in the industry, and that is money. Cloud computing is one thing which has provided a chance for small enterprises to reach the level of major players in the market.

Smaller organizations are able to accomplish much more despite investing significantly less capital through cloud computing, which makes them compete with not only SMEs but also the big organizations as well. As you move on to the next chapters, you will learn more about cloud computing, and it will become clearer to you why exactly most of the companies are considering moving towards the utilization of cloud computing services.

JAY A. COHEN

"And there's so much more to come. It's just the tip of the iceberg of what you can do for these kinds of technologies. ... It's the first inning. It might even be the first guy's up at bat. It's really early, and I think we're on the edge of a golden era."

-Jeff Bezos, CEO Amazon

Chapter 4
Big Cloud Players

Who would have thought that on-demand computing services would be the next big thing? It's like having a magic box with infinite storage and processing capabilities. The biggest benefactors of renting access to computing services are companies who do not need to pay high upfront costs of maintaining and setting up their own IT infrastructure. Cloud computing enables them to use what they want to use and pay for what they need. Since the advent and rise of cloud computing, there have been many who understood the potential of having economic benefits by making the computing services available to the public. However, there were even fewer who managed to cross the threshold and are now considered as the *"big three"* of cloud computing. Cloud computing pretty much covers every basic virtual service now, including natural language processing, basic storage, artificial intelligence, and office application services. All in all, if it's something related to the digital world, then you can find it on the cloud. It's no surprise that almost everyone is using this utility, but they have no idea what's it about and how it works, even though we have discussed it thoroughly in the previous chapters.

If you want to get familiar with the concept, then look around you and see the everyday services you use. We all know Netflix, right? But did you know that Netflix, one of the most popular media service provider company in the world, is also the 10th largest internet company by revenue? Netflix depends on the cloud for operations, including its video streaming services and so forth. Who are these "big three" and how did they take over the cloud to become the most successful computing vendors in the world?

Who Are The "Big Three" In The Cloud Computing World?

Needless to say, the ruling parties of the cloud computing world are all renowned names; Amazon, Google, and Microsoft Azure with Amazon taking the reins. These were the companies who denied those who said that cloud computing isn't going anywhere, but the market speaks otherwise. Let's dig deep on how, what, and why these companies are the big players of cloud computing.

Amazon

The name speaks for itself because Amazon is all set to give top IT companies a run for their money. And surprise, it's already doing that. Founded by Jeff Bozos in 1994, Amazon started as an online bookstore when the world was experiencing an internet boom. What started with selling books has now become the most sought out retailing platform in the world. Like every other success story, Bezos's Amazon didn't kick off well and oozed losses for the next six years after it became public in 1997. Note that this was a time when the world has gone crazy with the internet, and everybody is investing in anything that said "online." The losses didn't intimidate Bezos, and he continued to run the company by his famous "flywheel" philosophy of cutting back the prices (low prices) and focusing more on customer service. It's been a long run since then as Amazon hits the $1 trillion valuation. $1 trillion! It's not like Bezos did it by selling stuff but surprisingly, Amazon's Web Services provided the majority of the profits for the company and AWS has everything to do with cloud computing.

According to Amazon.com, Cloud Computing with Amazon web Services means, *"Amazon Web Services (AWS) is a secure cloud services platform, offering compute power, database storage, content delivery and other functionality to help businesses scale and grow. Explore how millions of customers are currently leveraging AWS cloud products and solutions to build sophisticated applications with increased flexibility, scalability and reliability."* Simply put, AWS offers the public with IaaS, and they were the first to do so. According to Techopedia, IaaS *"is a service model that delivers computer infrastructure on an outsourced basis to support enterprise operations. Typically, IaaS provides hardware, storage, servers and data center space or network components; it may also include software. Infrastructure as a service (IaaS) is also known as hardware as a service (HaaS)."*

In 2006, Amazon Web Services was officially launched with the combination of the three "S," also called S3, which offered cloud storage, EC2, and SQS. The mature thing that Amazon did was that it offered an extremely diversified amount of IaaS offerings. Furthermore, AWS has global coverage and largest number of data centers of any IaaS provider. As of today, AWS is powering thousands of business around the globe with reliable, safe, and cost-effective infrastructure platforms. Here's why Amazon is a success giant in cloud computing, as well as in the revenue race.

- Amazon considers itself as a platform that practices elasticity and agility when it comes to online services. AWS is a worldwide network of innovative, fast, and iterative cloud infrastructure. Amazon guarantees timesaving by instantly deploying new applications instead of waiting months for hardware.

This is a one-way lane towards rapid growth and an instant scale up and down based on demands. You need a dozen virtual servers, but you only use them a few hours in a day? No worries, as with AWS, you tend to pay for whatever you need depending on how much you use it.

- Low cost is the biggest asset of AWS, as the tech giant claims that their AWS provides pay-as-you-go low prices with long term commitment and close to no up-front expenses. They currently provide a gigantic network of a global infrastructure, which passes the cost-saving benefits in ways, including lower prices. Amazon claims that over the course of the past four years, they have been able to efficiently lower the prices on fifteen different occasions.
- Amazon considers flexibility as a viable asset and quality of AWS. The best thing about AWS is the freedom of choice and the variety of options available for choosing the programming or development model that best suits your needs. This is all so you can focus more on your work rather than getting hung up about the infrastructure.
- What's the most important thing an individual or a firm needs when they put their business and sensitive

data online? Security. Your services are a tad bit slow, and that's fine. However, if you can't provide a secure network, then that's a death sentence in cloud computing. Luckily, AWS is a platform where security is a priority, and it's a platform with durability and has certifications and audits from recognized industries. Amazon claims that the data is secure under tons of layers of operational and physical security.

Google Cloud

Google Cloud Platform was released on April 2008, as a platform that enabled users to develop and host web applications in data centers managed by Google. Google didn't kick off its public cloud services with infrastructure-as-a-service (IaaS), but instead, unlike Amazon and Microsoft Azure, Google started with Platform-as-a-Service (PaaS), which they called an App Engine. Even though the App Engine was announced to be released in 2008 by Google, but it wasn't until 2011, when it was made generally available for services. Experts say that relatively, Google is new in the field of cloud computing, but it's giving a tough competition to the other two of the "Big Three."

The App Engine was initially introduced to only 20,000 developers, which offered them a platform to utilize tools to run web applications on Google's infrastructure. At that time, the limitations were quite prominent because the developers could only use limited storage of 500 MB and the applications would only be written in Python. Furthermore, they could only use 10 GB bandwidth per day along with 200 million megacycles of CPU per day.

In May 2008, Google opened the signup of the App Engine preview to all developers. Alongside that, the search engine also announced API and Memcache. Though it was a breakthrough for Google, there was a complaint from developers that the platform didn't support Java, which is the most popular and basic programming language. Google responded to the critique by officially making the support for the Java programming language available. Jumping to May 2010, Google introduces Cloud Storage, which is its second major cloud service. This marked the official entry of Google in the IaaS market. Following Cloud Storage, Google also launches Google App Engine for Business. The app engine would go on to support features specifically used by big enterprises.

Finally, by November 2011, App Engine is launched as an official product from Google after it's taken out of preview. After that, it has been climbing the ladder of success. Even though Google hasn't been in the cloud computing business as long as its competitors, being the world's leading search engine has given it the advantages and credibility it needs. Google is able to deliver reliable cloud computing services to the public due to designing and managing web-scale data centers.

Google Cloud offers the following categories of cloud computing services. Even though these aren't enough as compared to Amazon and Microsoft Azure's extensive services portfolio, these tools have been specifically designed for developers that are hardly available on some other problem.

- **Storage and Database:** This category of cloud services include Cloud Storage object storage, Cloud Bigtable NoSQL database, Cloud Spanner relational database, Cloud SQL with MySQL database options, Cloud Datastore NoSQL database, and Persistent Disk block storage.
- **Compute:** Google Cloud Platform's compute includes the original cloud services of Google, the App Engine PaaS, Container Engine, Compute Engine, Container Registry, and Cloud Functions.
- **Big Data:** This category of services consists of Cloud Dataflow for stream and batch data

processing, BigQuery large-scale data warehouse, Cloud Datalab for analytics and visualizations, Cloud DataProc along with Spark and Hadoop capabilities, Cloud Pub/Sub messaging, Cloud Dataprep for data preparation, Google Data Studio for reporting business, and Genomics for genetic scientists.

- **Internet of Things (IoT):** This particular kind of cloud service from Google consists of Cloud IoT Core from Google, which is utilized for the management of a secure device connection.
- **Networking:** Networking category includes services related to Virtual Private Cloud (VPC), Cloud CDN content delivery, Cloud Load Balancing, Cloud DNS for Web domain serving, and providing Cloud Interconnect for connections of enterprise-grade to Google's Cloud.
- **Security:** Google's Cloud security includes Cloud Identity-Aware Proxy, Security Key Enforcement, Cloud IAM identity and access management, Cloud Data Loss Prevention API, Cloud Key Management Services, Cloud Security Scanner, and Cloud Resource Manager.

- **Management Tools:** The Management Tools category includes Monitoring and Logging, which supports both Google Cloud Platform and AWS, and also includes Stackdriver Overview. The Management Tools services from Google Cloud also offers beneficial cloud services for app optimization, alongside providing deployment tools which consist of Cloud Deployment Manager, Trace, Debugger, Cloud Mobile App, Cloud APIs, Cloud Billing API, Cloud Console, and Cloud Shell.
- **Machine Learning:** This Google Cloud Platform Services category includes APIs for natural language, speech, job search, translation, video intelligence, and vision, while it also includes Google's Cloud Machine Learning Engine.
- **Developer Tools:** This includes Gradle App Engine Plugin, Cloud SDK along with command-line interface for Google Cloud Platform services, Cloud Tools for Powershell, Cloud Tools for Eclipse, Maven App Engine Plugin, Cloud Source Repositories, Cloud Tools for Android Studio, Gradle App Engine Plugin, Cloud Test Lab for On-Demand Testing, and Cloud Tools for IntelliJ.

Even though there is an overwhelming amount of cloud

computing services from Google, however, there are a few instructions that include not considering Google as the first choice when it comes to organizations, which are right now moving legacy applications to the cloud. A survey by Cowen & Co. indicated that Google is priceless when it comes to cost, IT support, and customer service, but is probably a liability when it comes to security and compliance, which they claimed as one of its "weaknesses."

Microsoft Azure

Microsoft Azure was previously known as Windows Azure. It is Microsoft's official public cloud computing platform, which is in the run with AWS and Google Cloud, although it has more features than Google Cloud. Microsoft Azure offers an extensive range of cloud services, which include basic services like networking, storage, computing, and analytics. Microsoft Azure offers both, PaaS and IaaS. The first plans to introduce a cloud computing platform from Microsoft were first established way back in 2008, choosing to call it Windows Azure. The platform was released in its preview version until its official launch in 2010 to formally give some competition to Amazon Web Services, which was and is still running solidly on top. Even today, there are some services and aspects where businesses prefer Azure over Amazon for its distinct processing and outcomes functions.

Data and analysis suggest that the increasing number of Microsoft Azure users is due to the discount and credits that Microsoft offers on Azure. Azure's main focus lies in hybrid cloud computing, which is a group of private on-premises and off-premises public cloud services as compared to its competitors. This means that it is rather feasible for large companies to choose Azure because hybrid cloud setups are their main choice. So now, let's have a look at the services and products that are provided by Microsoft Azure.

Web: Microsoft Azure offers web services in order to support the deployment and development of web applications, content delivery application programming interface (API) management, reporting, and features for search and notifications.

Compute Services: This category of services includes the deployment and management of Virtual Machines (VMs), supporting remote application access as well as batch processing.

Networking: Like any other cloud computing service platform, Microsoft Azure offers a large group of virtual networks, gateways, load balancing, domain name system (DNS) hosting, dedicated connections, traffic management, network protection against distributed denial-of-service

(DDoS), and diagnostics.

Data Storage: This category involves the services of providing support for big data projects, scalable cloud storage for both unstructured and structured data, as well as maintained storage and archival storage.

Hybrid Integration: This service is the highlight of the platform, which is mainly a plus point for large corporations' usage. This category includes services for site recovery, server backup, and secure connection between public and private clouds.

Security: This category includes services providing abilities for identifying and immediately responding to security threats; including managing encryption keys and other sensitive assets.

Machine Learning and Artificial Intelligence (AI): Microsoft Azure has particularly put a lot of effort in improvising their network and services, which includes AI and cognitive computing abilities, which are incorporated in relevant applications and data sets. Also, Azure has a huge range of services for developers regarding machine learning.

Mobile: These services include a series of products for developers to build cloud applications for mobile devices following support for back-end-tasks, notification services, tools for developing APIs, and finally, coupling location context with data.

Migration: As discussed before, Microsoft Azure is the preferred platforms of corporate titans when it comes to migrating their entire workload. These kinds of tools are best suitable for an organization because it helps them estimate workload migration costs. It also helps them evaluate the actual workload displacement from the local data centers to the Azure Cloud.

Databases: These are the services which include database instances like Azure Cosmos DB, Database as a Service (DBaaS), Azure Database for PostgreSQL, SQL, NoSQL, caching, migration features, hybrid database integration, and SQL Data Warehouse support.

Even though these titans of the cloud computing platform have a strong foothold that cannot be shaken by the increasing number of competitors, companies like Oracle, IBM and Alibaba are already sweeping in numbers that can surpass the giants in the coming years. Trends suggest that the potential of cloud computing will continue to grow as there is plenty of room for AI. The world has only scratched the surface and there is still a lot more to offer, which can change the way we associate digitalization

JAY A. COHEN

"Overall, becoming a carbon-neutral country would involve changes in our behavior, but these are modest compared with the changes that will be forced upon us if we do nothing."

-Caroline Lucas

Chapter 5
Carbon Footprints

Can an organization today run without a data center? The simple answer to that question is *"No!"* With businesses expanding and things going digital, there's simply no way an organization can thrive without a well-equipped data center.

Defining Data Centers Briefly

For those who don't know, data centers are centralized locations where all the computing and networking equipment is arranged in order to collect, store, process, and distribute large amounts of data. The fact that might come to you as a shock is that data centers have existed in some form ever since the advent of computers. The data centers that we see in organizations today are simply an evolved version of the same thing. As computer equipment is getting cheaper and smaller and data processing needs of organizations are increasing exponentially over time, the tech people have no other reason but to network multiple servers. This is what increases the processing power of organizations these days, enabling them to communicate all over the world from remote locations.

Today, organizations house all their servers and other tech equipment in either a room or an entire building. Make no mistake, there are even organizations that are using groups of buildings to house their tech equipment these days. These servers are stacked in racks and arranged in rows. If an organization has a high concentration of servers in its data center, such organizations are said to have a server farm. These servers tend to run 24/7, which leads to the problem this chapter is dedicated to. They tend to consume a lot of energy, something we have already started to run out of. Simply put, the bigger a data center, the higher the consumption of energy.

The Electricity Consumed by Data Centers

According to research, the U.S. data centers consume more than 90 billion kW hours of electricity every single year. But that's not all that's shocking. That amount of energy requires 34 huge 500-megawatt coal-powered plants, give or take. Data centers of global organizations in the U.S roughly consume 416 terawatts. That's about three percent of all electricity produced in the country and forty percent more than the total energy consumption of the United Kingdom.

Here's some food for thought – that rate of energy consumption of data centers is set to double after every four years. It's a big problem as it is, and it's only going to get bigger with time. There was a time when people used to use a 3.8 GHz Pentium 4 that came out in 2004. Today, people don't want anything less than 3.8 GHz iCore i7. If Moore's Law is of any significance, the transistors are getting faster after every two years, making our computers work faster than ever. That means the computers we use today will be 8 times faster in 12 years. It doesn't take a genius to understand how fast the rate of energy consumption is increasing accordingly.

World's Most Energy-Consuming Data Centers

The energy consumed in data centers is measured in megawatts. Most people are unaware of the fact that data centers can be massive, and these massive things require an unimaginable amount of energy to power them. In order to understand the severity of this problem, let's take a look at some of the world's most energy-consuming data centers. You would be surprised to see that most of them are located in China. One of the reasons why so many data centers are located in China is cheap labor. Many multinationals have shifted their production facilities there to take advantage of this.

- **China Telecom – Inner Mongolia:** The data center of the Inner Mongolian Information Park is the one that consumes the largest amount of energy in the entire world. This data center is powered by not one but in fact several sources of energy, including hydroelectric and thermal power. Its size is about 10,763,910 square feet. Looking at the size of this data center, you can easily imagine the amount of energy it would consume – 150 megawatts of energy continuously.

- **China Mobile – Hohhot:** The Hohhot Data Center under the ownership of China Mobile ranks second in the list of the world's most energy-consuming data centers. Like the previous data center on the list, this one is powered by various energy sources, including, altitude, thermal power, and hydroelectric. Regardless, its continuous energy consumption is slightly lesser than the Inner Mongolian Information Park – consuming about 130 megawatts of energy.

- **China Mobile – Harbin:** This data center is located in Harbin, Heilongjiang. The Harbin Data Center happens to be the world's third-largest energy-consuming data center. This massive complex consumes up to 120 megawatts of energy.

- **Range – International Information Hub:** Here's an interesting fact about the Range International Information Hub – its size is the same as the Pentagon. It consumes 115 megawatts of energy and is currently the fourth largest energy-consuming data center. The purpose of this facility was to provide services to both government and private agencies. The facility was built in collaboration with IBM.

- **China Unicom – Northwest:** With an energy consumption rate of 110 megawatts of energy, China Unicom's Northwest Data Center makes it to the top five of this list. Its area is about 6,436,818 feet and building this facility cost China Unicom about 12.3 billion yuan. That amount is roughly equivalent to U.S $1.97 billion. Located in Hohhot, this data center is spread 78,740 feet below the ground.

- **China Mobile – Southern Logistics Center:** The fact that most energy-consuming data centers exist in China proves that the country would soon be hailed as the one that leaves the strongest carbon footprints on our environment. The China Mobile Southern

Data Center is built over 5,274,346 million square feet and the facility consumes 102 megawatts of energy. Like most data centers in China, this one too is located in Hohhot Inner Mongolia.

- **China Telecom – Guizhou Information Park:** For those who don't know, the Ghizhou Information Park is a recently added member of the China Telecom Data Center family. With its energy consumption of 100 megawatts, it easily takes the number seventh spot on this list. Building this data center was another expensive deal and it cost China Telecom nearly 7 billion yuan, which is equivalent to U.S $1.14 billion. One of the striking facts about this data center is that it is home to one million servers.

- **NSA Bumblehive:** The next largest energy-consuming data center in the world is NSA Bumblehive. This data center is not located in China, for a change. Instead, this data center is located in Bluffdale, Utah. It is the latest data center of the NSA and is referred to as the "The Country's Biggest Spy Center." Its energy consumption is about 90 megawatts and its square footage is about 1,100,000. The most interesting thing about this facility is that it consists of four separate data halls, each one of them having the square footage of 25,000. Moreover, each data hall has the capacity to house more than 1000 servers.

- **Digital Reality – Lakeside:** This data center, which is built on 1.1 million square feet, is unlike any other data center. Although its energy consumption is about 85 megawatts, the facility is home to more than 70 tenants with data centers for important businesses located in Chicago, including financial firms.
- **Tulip Telecom – Data City:** When Tulip Data City was inaugurated back in 2012, it was the third-largest data center in the world. The fact that its rank has now dropped to the world's tenth-largest energy-consuming data center shows how fast the size and energy consumption of data centers is increasing. Tulip Data City consumes 80 megawatts of energy. Its four towers cover around 900,000 square feet that consist of 20 Enterprise Modular Data Centers. Tulip Telecom Limited collaborated with IBM to build this facility so the company can support more than 2,000 locations it operates in India.

It shouldn't come to you as a shock that the sizes of data centers that are being built around the world are only going to increase over time. With just about every contemporary companies trying to capture the digital market, they are going to need larger data centers in the years to come. And as the size of these things increases, it's safe to assume that there will be a spike in energy consumption to power gigantic data centers as well.

Reasons Why Data Centers Consume High Energy

There are certain factors that make companies expand their data centers and add more servers to them. The biggest reasons of them all is video streaming. It won't be wrong to say that video streaming has changed the whole game, and things are about to get more intense in the years to come as the proliferation of artificial intelligence and internet-connected devices is predicted to shift everything by a great measure.

We all know artificial intelligence is the future we all have been waiting for quite some time now. AI is, without a doubt, processing power-hungry technology. And so is IoT. By 2020, IoT is expected to exceed 20 billion devices. In fact, there are a few analysts who believe that we will hit that number sooner than expected.

Currently, we have about 10 million IoT devices. If the number is about to double, you can very well imagine the kind of massive changes that organizations would have to do to the infrastructure of their data centers. It's perfectly normal to assume that would result in a huge increase in electricity consumption.

Data Centers and Global Warming

The use of excessive energy is bound to accelerate global warming. Yes, data centers are a threat to our environment. And the sad part is that we have grown so accustomed to using the latest technology that there's no turning back for us. We have limited options to cut back on the amount of energy that data centers are consuming.

According to an alarming new research, our failure to source renewable energy would end up making data centers one of the scariest polluters within the next 7 years. All organizations care about these days is adopting data-hungry machines that consume more power to keep the data centers running all over the world. It is obvious that drastic actions need to be taken to reduce their carbon footprint.

The Severity of Data Centers Polluting the World

The fact that should instill fear in our hearts is that the day when data centers are labeled the biggest electricity consumers is not very far. In fact, data centers are destined to become such a big polluter that they might leave the countries with a shockingly high energy consumption rate behind.

According to Climate Change News, the ICT industry will be responsible for up to 3.5 percent of global emissions by 2020 and that rate is expected to escalate to about 14 percent by 2040. The reason why the rate of global emissions will increase drastically in the years to come is that data centers will be consuming more than 20 percent of all electricity in the world by 2025, trying to create and distribute data at a speed so fast that it will leave people in awe. Analysts are of the opinion that the carbon footprint of data centers would amount to 5.5 percent of the global carbon footprint value in the years to come if efficient energy sources don't develop at speed.

The Options at Our Disposal to Reduce Carbon Footprints

Besides harnessing renewable energy sources, there is another remedy to prevent the escalation of energy consumption of data centers. That remedy is cloud computing! Various analysts point in the direction of cloud computing when it comes to figuring out what available options, we can use for controlling the energy being consumed at data centers all over the world.

Can Cloud Computing Help?

The simplest answer to that question is *"Yes!"* Cloud computing can reduce the consumption of energy globally by 38 percent. Many studies suggest that the increase in the use of cloud computing technology is key to reducing the energy consumption of data centers from the existing rate of 201.8 terawatt-hours to 139.8 terawatt-hours by 2020. Not just that. The use of cloud computing will also result in a reduction in greenhouse gas emissions within the next five years.

A recent study conducted by Accenture for Microsoft compared the environmental impacts of Microsoft's three business applications, namely Exchange, Dynamic CRM, and SharePoint that are used in Microsoft cloud data centers and customer data centers. The study concluded that Microsoft cloud data centers reduced carbon emissions. The results stated that Microsoft cloud data centers reduced carbon emissions by 90 percent or more for small operations (per 100 users), 60 percent to 90 percent for medium-sized operations (per 1,000 users), and 30 percent to 60 percent for large operations (per 10,000 users). The problem is that, currently, organizations lack the motivation for using green energy. Not many organizations care about becoming good corporate citizens. However, some awareness has led government entities, like the European Union Emissions Trading Scheme (EU ETS) and the State of California, to propose regulations in order to reduce carbon emissions. The basic reason why cloud data centers are able to save energy is that they achieve really high virtualization ratios, especially if the cloud data center is using new and efficient equipment.

How Cloud Computing Can Reduce Carbon Footprint

Only a few people know the fact that IT accounts for about 2 percent of greenhouse gas emissions in the entire world. As businesses heavily rely on tech equipment, like computers, laptops, and other similar technologies, the demand for a more sustainable IT has become a dominating trend.

One of the easiest ways to conserve energy used in data centers is to use cloud computing. The reason why cloud technology has become so popular is that it allows organizations to outsource programs over the internet to service providers. Another benefit of using cloud computing is that replaces heavy tech equipment with virtual services, such as data storage and video streaming.

Cloud Computing for More Sustainable IT

Cloud computing has become an essential feature of IT environmental sustainability. The reason being, cloud computing addresses two highly critical elements that are conducive to green IT – resource efficiency and energy efficiency. According to Google research, organizations can effectively save up to 60 to 85 percent of their energy costs if they switch to cloud computing.

It so happens that cloud technology uses energy in a way that is more streamlined and cleaner than traditional in-house data centers. The simplest example to give at this point is the cloud's virtual storage space. It completely eliminates the need for purchasing storage hardware that organizations must keep storing large volumes of data. According to a study commissioned by the Carbon Disclosure Project (CDP), just by reducing the number of hardware required for storing data would prevent 85.7 million metric tons of carbon emissions every year by 2020.

In short, corporations that have invested in cloud computing can reduce their carbon footprints by 95 percent. That is a huge percentage when compared to companies that have not decided in favor of cloud computing and still prefer to keep servers on their premises. Cloud computing is a perfect option for all those companies that intend to go green by taking a step toward reducing their carbon footprints and protecting the environment.

JAY A. COHEN

"Line-of-business leaders everywhere are bypassing IT departments to get applications from the cloud (also known as software as a service, or SaaS) and paying for them like they would a magazine subscription. And when the service is no longer required, they can cancel that subscription with no equipment left unused in the corner."

-Daryl Plummer, Managing Vice President and Distinguished Analyst at Gartner

Chapter 6
Capital and Operating Expenses

Why are companies building gigantic data centers when they are simpler options available? The number and sizes of data centers that are being built today are definitely not reducing. Delving a little deeper into this conundrum would give us the answer to the above question. The fact of the matter is that companies still don't have faith in outsourcing their data centers to third parties and they really have not opened up to the idea of investing in cloud computing yet. If you ask the CIO or CTO of a major multinational company why they need a data center at their company's premises, they are likely to give the following reasons:

- The company's data is very sensitive. Therefore, the company cannot take the risk of storing the data in a data center that is built and managed by a third party.
- The company already owns the main equipment that is required to set up a data center. So building a complete full-fledged data center is not a very expensive option for the company.

- They simply don't approve of available options, such as cloud computing, colocation, or data center leasing. The main reason why they don't approve of these options is that they don't know much about these options.
- The company simply doesn't care about contaminating the environment and it has tons of money to waste.

Companies that stay abreast with the latest advancements in the tech world know for a fact that cloud computing is safe. In fact, there are better ways to protect your data on the cloud. They also know that going digital is the future, which is why they make the smart decision of investing in it.

Besides saving the environment, there are other benefits of adopting cloud computing. With cloud computing, companies don't have to worry about running applications and programs from downloaded software on their servers and computers. People can access the same applications over the internet, which cut their operational and capital expenses.

The use of cloud computing has become so prevalent that you can't even keep a count of how many times in a single day you use the cloud services. When you send or receive an email, you are in the cloud. When you write a Facebook post, you are in the cloud. When you check your bank balance on your phone, you are using the cloud service again.

Such services make it easy for businesses, especially the small ones, to manage their day to day operations and help them overcome challenges related to managing workload. Cloud computing has already become the new standard. Almost 90 percent of businesses in the UK are using at least one cloud service today. One of the reasons why so many companies are shifting to cloud computing is because it is considerably more diverse than the fact that cloud computing helps reduce carbon emissions and saves the environment.

Before moving on to how cloud computing can cut your operating and capital expenses, it's best that you first try to understand just how expensive building a data center can be for a company.

How Much Does Building and Maintaining a Data Center Cost?

It's imperative for businesses to know that building a data center and maintaining it requires both money and expertise. If your company has enough money to build and maintain its own data center, but it doesn't have talented professionals to maintain it and keep it functional, then building a data center is definitely not a good option for your company. Obviously, the cost of building a data center depends on the size of the facility that you need to build. For the sake of this argument, let's assume that a company wants to build a data center that has a square footage of 1,000. If the cost of building a data center is $1,000 per square foot, the facility is going to cost the company $1 million.

And if the company is planning on building a data center that is as big as the data centers of Google and Facebook, then the company must set aside at least $250 million to $500 million. Now, that's a huge capital expenditure that is not even possible for a normal, financially sound corporation. Not even a thorough cost-benefit analysis would be able to sanction building a data center that expensive.

How Cloud Computing Cuts Operating and Capital Expenses?

Cloud computing has indisputably revolutionized the corporate world. Indeed, it's safe to say that cloud technology is the most drastic disruptive innovation we have experienced in recent times since the advent of the internet. Here's how cloud computing can reduce a company's operational and capital expenditures:

No Need to Purchase a Data Center Building

One of the biggest expenses that a company is required to incur is purchasing a building where its data center will be housed. Even if a company owns a building that can be used for the stated purpose, it will have to bear several heavy expenses, including power and network connections.

No Storage Units and Servers

Building a private data center means the company will have to purchase all the costly equipment, which includes storage devices and servers. However, if you opt for cloud computing, your company can steer clear of these expenses.

Software Licenses

Unless you want to use the pirated software, you have to pay for the original ones. Companies end up spending millions of dollars on purchasing software and their licenses. Believe it or not, companies need several licenses and software to run a data center.

Energy Costs

Energy cost is perhaps the biggest operating expense that a company has to bear if it wants to establish a fully functional data center at its own premises. The energy consumption of a data center depends on its size. There's no denying the fact that the energy costs can be as high as $100,000 per megawatt. Besides that, you would have to add backup power equipment, so the functionality of your company's data center is not compromised in case there's a power breakdown or a technical fault.

Network Connectivity

The next big expense is network connectivity. If a data center requires one mile of fiber optic, it might cost the company around $250,000. It's a hefty expense for sure.

Cooling Equipment

A data center cannot work with a proper cooling system installed inside the facility. A data center tends to produce a lot of heat that needs to be taken out of the facility in order to prolong the life of all the equipment.

The Benefits of Cloud Computing for Startups and Small Companies

Cloud computing is nothing short of a miracle for small-scale businesses. With cloud computing, small companies and startups can think big and aim for achieving targets that were impossible to achieve before.

Cloud Makes a Company Flexible

Cloud-based services are ideal for companies with fluctuating or growing bandwidth needs. Startups cannot afford fully equipped data centers. With cloud computing, it gets easier for such companies to scale their bandwidth capacity up or down according to their immediate needs.

Cloud Makes Disaster Recovery Easy

Startups and small businesses are usually short on cash and expertise. That makes it very difficult for them to invest in a robust disaster recovery program. Thanks to cloud computing, such organizations now have an option to recover their lost data in case their premises encounter a disaster.

Automatic and Cost-Effective Software Updates

The best thing about cloud computing is that its servers are offsite. Companies that are on a budget cannot always afford expensive updates for software that they use. Cloud computing makes it easier for them to work on the latest versions of the software without having to spend any money.

Spares a Company from Purchasing Hardware

Purchasing hardware equipment for storage purposes and for servers is a costly capital expense. In fact, it's not just buying the equipment that is costly as maintaining it is equally expensive. If you are running a business with tight cash flow, you can resort to using cloud computing and spare yourself from investing in all the expensive hardware.

Cloud Computing Increases Online Collaboration

Think about how much money a company can save if its

employees can share, edit, and access documents and information anytime from anywhere. This feature of cloud computing makes it easier for small businesses and startups to do more and do it in a better way. With the help of file sharing apps and cloud-based workflow, it allows people to manage their work in real-time.

Cloud Computing Makes Expansion Easier

Small companies and startups can dream big now. Cloud computing has enabled them to think of expanding their business on regional, national, and international scales. Before the advent of cloud computing, expanding a business meant hiring more experts and professionals who could take care of the business operations in other cities and countries. Other input costs were also substantial. Now, you don't have to think that way. Fewer people can manage the business and see its operations from anywhere in the world. Now, all companies need to have is the internet for expanding their operations. You can imagine the amount of money companies can save if they intend to extend their business.

Cloud Computing Is Safe and Secure

Companies spend millions of dollars on the security of their data. And they should for all the good reasons. Data security is perhaps the single most important thing for firms today. But what about the companies that are struggling financially and cannot afford the same quality of data security? This is where cloud computing comes into play.

You don't have to be concerned about company laptops being stolen or a virus destroying the hard drives when your data is safely stored in the cloud. Even if the most dangerous virus affects your laptop, you can still access your data. Moreover, you can wipe data from your laptops if they get lost to guarantee your company's sensitive information does not get into the wrong hands.

Cloud Computing Makes a Company Competitive

It's not easy to bring your business up to the latest standards to give your business rivals a competition. Cloud computing is the technology that allows businesses to upgrade their operational efficiency without having to spend a substantial amount of money. If truth be told, there's no better way to gain access to enterprise-class technology than cloud computing. The best feature about cloud computing is that it allows small businesses to compete with bigger and more established businesses at the same level.

The Virtual Services Offered by Cloud Computing

Planning on switching to cloud computing is a wise decision for many reasons. We have already discussed those reasons in the paragraphs above. It's time to take a look at virtual services that companies can benefit from if they choose to switch to cloud computing:

- Outsource processes
- Offline access
- Online storage
- Online office
- Shared calendars
- Online resources
- Third-party integration
- Online collaboration

So, why build a data center when you have cloud computing? Building a data center and maintaining it can be a tedious and expensive task. Come to think of it; it can cost a company millions of dollars. However, the same companies can save their money by switching to cloud computing technology. That way, these companies wouldn't have to spend millions on building a data center. The cloud computing service can allow the users to use online storage free of cost.

Usually, when companies are told that there exists an option that can save their money, they take notice of that without fail. Cloud computing happens to be one of those options as well whose use can lead companies to save their money. The reason why cloud computing saves money is because it involves the use of cleantech applications, such as data storage, smart grids, and other virtual services that are designed to drive down energy resources and keep IT costs low. Moreover, they provide your organization with more efficient management options. Cloud computing also cuts operational cost because it reduces data running, the time required for computing, and other related expenses. Moreover, cloud computing promotes online collaboration, which almost eliminates the need for conducting fact-to-face corporate meetings. In fact, the report issued by the CDP states that American companies can save up to $12 billion by making a wise decision and investing in cloud computing.

After all, it makes sense. When cloud computing eliminates the need for purchasing all the required server equipment and hardware for storage purposes, it also cuts the cost for maintaining the equipment and regularly upgrading it.

What Is Better for a Growing Company – Building a Data Center or Cloud Computing?

Businesses that are in the growth phase need additional storage space for their data and more applications for email or streaming. This is when companies need to choose between building an in-house data center and opting for cloud computing. Making this decision depends on several things, including the following:

How Much Is Your Business Expected to Grow?

In this day and age, business owners wish to expand their businesses in all four corners of the world. But that kind of expansion does not happen overnight. It takes time. Cloud computing is good enough for companies that are experiencing growth. However, keeping the cost of building a data center in mind, it's better to rely on cloud computing unless your business becomes as big as Google or Facebook.

The Kind of Expertise Your Company Has?

Like we discussed earlier in this chapter, a company needs to have professionals to maintain a data center. Most startups don't have that kind of talent. Thus, they should opt for cloud computing until they require a more sophisticated data center of their own.

What Level of Security Does Your Company Need?

Companies need to guard their data at all costs. And for that, companies need to invest a significant amount of money in securing their data centers. That's why the idea for building a data center is better suited for large multinationals, not small companies or startups. The level of security that a startup or a small-scale company needs are easily provided by cloud computing. In fact, medium-sized companies today also rely on cloud computing.

The Kind of Control You Need Over the Data

Usually, companies end up building in-house data centers because they want total control over their data. They don't want to trust a third-party when it comes to keeping their data secure and private. However, a growing company does not need to worry about that. Growing companies should be more cost-effective, and that they should realize their data is entirely secure on the cloud.

Summing this chapter up, there's no better option than cloud computing for small-scale companies and startups. It's simply perfect for them. It's a cost-effective option by all means. Also, cloud computing can address several challenges related to workflow and data management, which are faced by small and medium-sized companies as they continue to grow

JAY A. COHEN

"I don't need a hard disk in my computer if I can get to the server faster... carrying around these non-connected computers is byzantine by comparison."

-Steve Jobs, Late Chairman and Co-Founder of *Apple*

Chapter 7
Total Cost of Ownership

If you want to understand why cloud computing has started to take over the traditional data centers, you will have to delve a little deeper and explore some essential ground realities. This chapter will walk you through one of the biggest reasons why cloud computing has almost replaced the concept of building in-house data centers. But first, let's just get into the basics to build the base of this chapter.

For the last few decades, companies are in the habit of building huge data centers in their buildings. These centralized locations are where computer relevant resources and data are stored. Of course, the users do not require some kind of physical access to use these resources. It's not necessary that all data centers should be equally big. They can be built in small rooms and others might decide to co-locate with other companies in a big data center as well. But most organizations, especially the big ones, prefer to build data centers on a floor of a building, or even the entire building.

Well, have you dared to imagine the cost of building a

data center that is so big that it occupies an entire building? There are large oversized doors leading to such data centers. Then, there's a loading dock, ramps, and service elevators. Now that doesn't look like a normal or ordinary investment. It's a huge decision if a company wants to build a data center that big and invest a colossal sum of money in something that is practically on the verge of getting replaced by something more convenient, smart, and cost-effective.

Having an in-house data center increases the risk of natural disasters ruining it. Companies can completely collapse if their data centers are damaged, let alone destroyed, because of unforeseen events like earthquakes, floods, lightning, fire, and hurricanes. And such calamities have destroyed data centers in the past. So, what does that mean? It means if you have made up your mind to build a data center in your office building, you better get ready to invest in a backup facility as well. Important safe guards must also be installed. You know that translates to another heavy capital expenditure.

It's either that or you have to arrange for really high-tech fire protection, weight rated floor, access to power, access to HVAC, and other access controls so your data center stays protected and unharmed at all times. Come to think of it, that's not very inexpensive either. If you dare to go cheap on safety arrangements, you know mishaps never give you a warning before they strike you. Hence, you can expect an emergency to arise at the most inopportune moment.

Protecting your data center from unforeseen events is not enough. You have to keep it secure from the internal and external threats as well, and that means more cost. Moreover, you will have to build a data center that has crime prevention facilities installed in it, like fences, walls, gates, natural barriers, surveillance, and alarms, etc. Besides all that, you will have to make sure there are appropriate physical security measures. For instance, limited access is one security measure. You have to make sure that access to the data center is on a need to be their basis only. For that, you will need keycards, old-fashioned keys and locks, biometric passes, and proximity badges.

At this point, you must be struggling to keep track of everything that is needed. Look at all the fuss that is involved with running an in-house data center. And that's just the fuss related to the security of an in-house data center. There are lots of other things that you need to focus on before you decide on building an in-house data center, like operating expenses.

Apart from the massive cost of building a data center, a

company also has to bear a huge cost for its operating expenses. A large portion of these operating expenses are attributed to the electricity bill. Then, you have to pay for the IT staff. In addition to that, you'd have to pay a significant amount for the permits and licenses. Let's explore these expenses in detail and see why they are considered so substantial.

Measuring the Total Cost of Ownership for Data Centers

Calculating or predicting the total cost of ownership, i.e. TCO, for the whole infrastructure of data centers and network rooms is very important for return on investment (ROI) analysis. In fact, it's good to have those calculations done when it's time to make big and important business decisions. The physical infrastructure of data centers includes all of the equipment at the facility that is needed to provide power, physical protection, and cooling. As it turns out, there are no proper methods to calculate the total cost of ownership of data centers. The best way is to add together the operating and capital expenses associated with operating data centers.

Several pieces of research have been conducted in order to figure out what the cost of running an in-house data center is, and almost all of them have, more or less, given similar results. Studies show that a typical data center is only utilized to 30 percent of its capacity. On the other hand, you can easily come across several data centers that are utilized up to 90 percent or more of their total capacity. Some small companies and startups that have their private data centers reportedly utilize their data centers up to only 10 percent of their total capacity. The percentages of data centers' utilization vary during the lifetime of a data center. This means that a data center is never used consistently throughout its lifetime.

For the purpose of explaining to you how and why in-house data centers are so expensive, let's take a comprehensive example that should make things easy for you. The center of this example will be a data center with the following characteristics:

- Power rating: 100kW
- Power density: 50 W/sq. ft
- Life cycle: 10 years
- Average rack power: 1,500 W
- Redundancy: 2N

This example is focused on a very small data center to keep the calculation nice and easy. However, this example can be used as a base to project the total cost of ownership of a typical data center. According to the research, the total cost of ownership for this particular data center will be approximately $120K over the data center's lifetime. This cost includes all the capital expenses and operating expenses, which combined amount almost 50 percent of this cost. An estimated breakup of the total cost of ownership for the data center is something like this:

- Electricity is the costliest expense. It is about 20 percent of the total cost of ownership.
- Power equipment is about 18 percent of the total cost of ownership.
- Engineering and installation expenses are also about 18 percent of the total cost of ownership.
- Arranging for space for the data center is about 15 percent of the total cost of ownership.
- Fiber optic service is also about 15 percent of the total cost of ownership.
- The cooling equipment is about 6 percent of the total cost of ownership.
- The management of the data center is about 5 percent of the total cost of ownership.
- Other expenses, like system monitoring and racks, are about 1 percent and 2 percent.

The point of giving this example is that if a small data center costs that much, it's almost impossible for a small company or a startup to invest that kind of money in a data center that is going to cost more than $120k. It's highly unfeasible for startups because, obviously, they will require a bigger data center than the one mentioned in the example. Furthermore, if by any chance, the company decides on expanding its operations, the company will need an even bigger data center to meet the needs of the business.

All these operating expenses can be easily avoided by using cloud computing servers. That's the latest thing, and it's slowly taking over the traditional idea of building data centers in your organization. Still, multinationals and big corporations go for in-house data centers, even though startups and small and medium-sized companies have started to opt for cloud computing services for a million reasons. For instance, you won't need any fiber-optic service, you won't need space to build a data center, you won't have to hire tech people to design and run your data center, you won't have to pay tech staff, your electricity bill will be normal, and you won't even have to pay for permits and licenses. Sounds super convenient, doesn't it? For the purpose of this argument, let's try to find out why it's so cost-effective to opt for cloud computing services.

Understanding Why Cloud Computing Is

All the Rage

If you take a look at Gartner studies and Forrester studies, you will come to notice one thing – 84 percent of CIOs report that they have cut application costs by moving to the cloud. The purpose of this statistical fact is to enable you to make reasonable arguments, depending on your place in the marketplace. Hence, the big question we're trying to deal with here is whether or not cloud computing is cost-effective. To answer that question, let's explore some basic facts.

Hardware

The biggest cost-saving feature of cloud computing is that you don't have to allocate money on hardware equipment. Hardware equipment can include anything from a storage area network to any other hardware found in a traditional environment, like your router switches. In general, public cloud solutions do not require the outright purchase of server hardware or network storage. You don't even need backup systems. The backup systems are inherent to a public cloud environment from a subscription perspective. The same thing can be said about disaster recovery systems. The one important thing to notice in the cloud space and any cloud environment is that the disaster recovery goes through a variety of options.

We all know that disaster recovery is not just isolated to the physical hardware. The other side of it pertains to the power and cooling systems as well. When we talk about power systems used in data centers, we're looking at large-scale Liebert battery systems, and dual power feeds, duplicate grids or redundant grid feeds within the electrical space. The maintenance cost associated with these things is pretty high, and you get to avoid all those costs if you're wise and smart enough to opt for the cloud services. Cloud computing increases the security maintenance and efficiency of your computers.

As a result of this, the life of your computers will increase, the depreciation costs will decrease, and technological obsolescence will slow down. From a hardware perspective, when you go into a cloud environment, one of the cost-effective arguments is that you're not required to upgrade the hardware with the rapidity that you would while housing this and hosting this locally. You will be able to take advantage of the different virtualization elements that the data center provider brings to the table.

You won't be suffering from any technology stagnation that frequently manifests when you make an investment on the capital expenditures' side. In fact, many organizations have reported that cloud computing allows them to take advantage of higher-end resources and higher cost resources that may not be financially feasible otherwise. Moreover, cloud services mitigate some of the risk factors in the hardware environment, like the infiltration standpoint placement of malware and any other element that can potentially compromise the hardware itself.

Software

Buying software for your own data center is a costly expense. However, cloud computing spares you from incurring that expense. No licenses and no permits are required in cloud computing. In fact, you don't have to worry about the latest versions of software and updates. All the software on the cloud gets updated automatically. Automatic software updates remove the cost of constantly purchasing, running, and maintaining new software versions. Courtesy to this, users get to work on the latest versions of the software you use. There's no better way of improving the efficiency of your business operations with the help of the latest software versions. Indeed, users who move apps to the cloud save 21 percent a year on average.

The cloud services allow users to decrease reliance on local developers and software resources. The users don't have to worry about upgrading and renewing licenses as well. All these elements come into play when you're talking about potential cost reductions and technological improvements. When companies move from software to a service model, they take advantage of virtualization at the provider level. Many companies have started to offset the cost associated with SaaS by addressing revenue increases and the revenue attainment through the expansion of the business and addressing cultural and demographic obstacles. They are taking advantage of new opportunities now. For instance, there's a French cosmetic company that wanted to expand its market into the Chinese space.

The company didn't have the resources for expansion, so the company engaged a software service provider. Thanks to their help, the French firm entered the Chinese market and experienced a tremendous amount of growth. This way, the French company overcame the development challenges, language barriers, and cultural barriers – all by setting up and maintaining a data center in China. With cloud computing, the company was able to overcome staffing considerations, management consideration, and other hassles that come with it.

Support & Maintenance

There is no fixed support and maintenance cost when you opt for cloud services. The support and maintenance cost completely depend on your needs in that space and the level of control that you wish to exercise. In a typical public cloud environment, the cloud provider monitors, maintains, and upgrades all hosted programs. It stores data and increases the capabilities within your storage area network sources and environments. Public cloud environment runs regular data backup and redundancy, handling all backup costs and fees. All these features allow companies build huge data centers, which are sometimes as big as 200,000 square feet.

IT Personnel

There are some actual hard dollars associated with employment considerations when you are running an in-house data center. But you don't need tech staff when you have shifted to the cloud services. Companies that use the cloud to deploy their applications spend 25 percent less on personnel, and that's a huge saving. It's considerable cost-cutting for companies. In fact, that's the best feature of cloud computing. Come to think of it; a company needs to hire an army of employees to take care of their in-house data center. They need employees for hardware maintenance, software licensing, deployment considerations, and addressing backups. With cloud computing, more than 62 percent of companies that are saving IT personnel costs are reinvesting those savings back into the business to increase their headcount in other relevant and important areas of the business, like sales, operations, and customer support service.

With the amount of money that a company saves by adopting cloud solutions, it can boost the wages of employees and give them better incentives. Moreover, last but not least, organizations prefer to reinvest the money saved into driving product innovation.

That means they reinvest money in research and development to bring innovation to their existing products and introduce an innovative line of products that serves the needs and wants of the end customers. In fact, companies now have a better chance to allocate more space or increase the space for production. All those people who are familiar with supporting an in-house data center environment locally can attest to the fact that companies not only have hardware costs to meet but must also have the human resources needed to support them, which in itself is a considerable expense as well. Then, there are related storage considerations. Some of the companies may still be using tape backups.

But when you're looking at the cloud solutions and associated costs, companies that are smart and prudent know they are making a better decision. They know they are making a better investment with their dollars. The servers of cloud computing services are offsite and are readily accessible. As such, there was a company that lost its access to its disaster recovery location for over two weeks. With the director of IT of that company being overseas at the time, they had no option but to turn to cloud solutions.

There were several considerations to look into before the cloud service company could advise appropriate action to them. Sure, there were connectivity issues, but there were some other pretty serious considerations as well. For starters, the company was hosting all its applications, its software needs, and all its production elements, in its in-house singular environment. The cloud service company took care of its data center. Now, the company has its daily backups, and it has access to the various programs it needs in the event of any disaster.

The Cost and Benefit Analysis

To get across the message clearly, let's examine the cost and benefit analysis of a traditional data center and cloud computing. The following cost and benefit analysis is based on 150 employees over 5 years. A company has 150 employees and decides to build a local data center.

The following will be the cost of the facility that the company will have to incur in terms of hardware costs, software costs, support, infrastructure, and IT personnel:

150 personal computers costing about $800 each, space for data center allocated to each user at the rate of $200, email and other software needs (about $10 per user), backup costs (about $13 per user), at least three servers (about $5,000 each), and 6 IT personnel (about $75,000 each). The cost of that kind of facility will be more than $2 million. That is not the kind of expense a startup or a small-to-medium-sized company can incur without thinking the whole idea through. It's not even feasible for the company to incur that kind of expense when it becomes financially sound. On the other hand, consider if the same company opts for cloud solutions. With the same number of employees and for 5 years, the total expense for the company would be a little more than $700,000.

This brief and simple example pretty much demonstrates it all. The math in this example is easy, and you can see for yourself that cloud computing saves money considerably. The same money can be reinvested by the company in areas that need further improvement or better personnel. Saving that kind of money is a blessing for a startup. It allows the company to think about areas that need more attention.

The cost and benefit analysis above incorporate all the factors that are discussed in this chapter – hardware, software, support, infrastructure, and IT personnel. It gives you a true and fair view of how traditional in-house data centers can be compared with a newer and easier alternative – that is cloud computing. This assessment is based on only 150 employees. But it's enough to give an idea of how the costs will multiply if the number of employees will increase. The idea was to show you that despite making some cost adjustments, local or in-house data centers are a luxury that most companies cannot afford. Even if the cost of building and maintaining and running local data centers is cut to half, it's still a pretty sizable investment as opposed to what you're being offered on the cloud.

Some large organizations are okay with a capital expenditure of that sort. It all comes down to your company's needs and size and which option is going to provide you with the most output for your dollar. Also, before deciding in favor of these two options, you also need to address all the considerations that are discussed in this chapter.

With cloud computing, some of the smaller entities might be able to get into higher-end hardware environments that they wouldn't be able to finance otherwise in a capital expenditure (capex) environment. Smaller entities might be looking towards IT staff and supplementing that staff because of their budgetary considerations, but cloud computing allows these companies to minimize their operating expenses related to tech staff easily. So much so, small-scale companies need not worry about upgrading their software after every 12 to 24 months because the cloud solutions offer them with automatic updates as opposed to having somebody go through and do so manually, and then have someone else go through the renewal process in the contract management.

Moreover, the monitoring elements that come with cloud computing enable users to monitor their business operations remotely. Not just that, the advanced cloud computing solutions also enable companies to manage their operations remotely and rapidly. The speed at which the users can manage their operations via cloud solutions does not imply that cloud computing doesn't offer security. Cloud computing ensures both security and efficiency at the same time, which makes it the optimal IT solution – especially for startups and small and medium-sized companies.

JAY A. COHEN

"The appeal of wearable technology is down to the rich data generated by the devices, which is stored and analyzed in the cloud. The ability to access these insights from the cloud – anywhere, anytime -enables wearable technology users to boost their intelligence, confidence, health, fitness and even their love lives"

-Drs. Chris Brauer and Jennifer Barth, Centre for Creative and Social Technology (CAST)

Chapter 8
The Benefits of Cloud Computing

With time, things are becoming easier and easier every day. So far, in this book, we have established the fact that not only is cloud computing the latest alternative to traditional data centers, but that it has also made IT-related operations simpler and cost-effective. In fact, the cost-effectiveness of cloud solutions is so tempting that it has allowed businesses to explore new dimensions – even if they don't have the required resources and capital to invest. Suffice to say, cloud computing is the best and most useful breakthrough in the world of IT since the internet. It has changed the world drastically, as well as the way people do business these days. Speaking on behalf of startups and small and medium-sized companies (SMEs), cloud computing is like a dream come true. Come to think of it, startups and small-sized companies are not that wrong. Cloud computing has provided them with options they couldn't even think of a couple of decades ago.

In fact, cloud computing has made small and medium-sized companies compete with financially sound and established companies. In some cases, these small companies have left multinationals behind. That means, with the help of cloud computing, startups are expanding their businesses at a faster rate than some of the big companies working in the same industry. To refresh your memory and to get your juices flowing, let's briefly discuss how cloud computing works and how it has created ease for businesses.

What Is Cloud Computing All About?

Organizations today have a lot of stuff, and that's not their fault. That's how business operations have evolved. Today, businesses have data stored in all sorts of formats. They have applications, document files, audio files, video files, podcasts, eBooks, and a lot of other things. To explain cloud computing in the simplest terms, let's imagine a brief and simple hypothetical scenario.

A business that has loads of data stored in all these formats happens to be constantly struggling with a single problem – finding space to store all that data. In fact, the amount of data that modern-day companies have is so much that it has become next to impossible for them to store all of it physically. If truth be told, all of that has happened after the advent of the internet. But the solution to the prevailing problem is also internet-based.

There was once a time when people used to believe that storing data in virtual territory was purely science fiction. But it's not science fiction anymore. Cloud computing has proved that something like that actually exists. There, I said it. You must have guessed that the solution to the problem mentioned above is cloud computing. It is true that cloud computing is the best way to store all your data. There's absolutely no need to build huge data centers for that purpose, especially if your company is a startup or small-sized company. It's time to move on to modern and easier solutions. Besides storage space, cloud computing provides solutions to other diverse problems as well. In fact, those solutions are for their benefit as well. And that's what we'll discuss in this chapter.

With cloud computing, all your stuff can be stored on the internet space of the World Wide Web, instead of the limited space of your computer hard drives. Cloud computing was best described in Johnathan Strickland's article. He stated the pervasive impact of cloud computing in the following manner: *"The versatility and power of cloud computing is having a profound impact in the corporate setting and on personal computing."*

That's actually true, and with time, the impact of cloud computing on corporate sector and personal computing is only getting stronger and stronger.

How Does Cloud Computing Work?

Storing data and applications on remote servers and accessing them via the internet rather than saving or installing them on your personal or office computer is known as cloud computing. It allows you to store all your data, regardless of its format. Of course, this is amazing, but ever wondered why the term "cloud" means in cloud computing? The word "cloud" is used because data and applications are stored on a collection of web servers and computers owned by a third-party somewhere else. And that somewhere else is actually a remote location situated miles and miles away from you.

The cloud can be accessed via the cloud computing system interface software. That can be as simple as using a web-based service, which hosts all the applications and files that you would need for your job or your personal life. The cloud is being used not only to store data, but also as an inexpensive, efficient, and flexible alternative to purchasing, running, and maintaining in-house computing equipment and software. Not only that, the cloud gives you the ability to work anywhere at any time because all the information you need is always at your fingertips. One easy example of cloud computing is an online email account. When you use your online email accounts, like Hotmail and Gmail, you log into a web email account remotely through a browser, but the storage for your account doesn't exist on your computer. It belongs on the email provider's cloud.

Now that you understand what a cloud computing system is, let's move on to understanding how your data is stored on the cloud. The cloud computing architecture is comprised of two parts – the front end and the back end. Both these parts are connected by the internet.

The Front End of the Cloud Computing Architecture

The front end represents the computer that you as a client see. This side requires you to access the cloud computing system. Gaining access can be as simple as using an internet browser or as complex as using a unique interface software that lets you access the cloud.

The Back End of the Cloud Computing Architecture

The back end of a cloud computing system is comprised of the computers, servers, and data storage systems, which store all your files and information. This is the part that does all the technical work. There is a central server that administers the system monitoring traffic and client demands to ensure everything runs smoothly. In addition to that, this central server follows a set of rules known as protocols. The central server also uses a software called middleware that allows the network computers to communicate with each other.

Naturally, cloud computing companies have a built-in redundancy where they save multiple copies of your work in case of problems. However, the more clients they have, the more storage space they need. Due to this, cloud computing companies require at least twice the number of storage devices to store their clients' information.

Why People Choose Cloud Computing

The answer to that question is the many benefits of cloud computing. Owing to the numerous advantages, people end up choosing cloud computing as a viable option for data storage because its applications are limitless.

The Benefits of Cloud Computing

Let's start with the basic benefits of cloud computing and save the complex for the last. A cloud computing user enjoys the following benefits:

1- Provide the Ease of Accessing Your Data from Anywhere

Cloud computing allows you to access your application and data from anywhere. It doesn't make a difference what kind of file you want to access. All you have to do is make a few clicks and access your data at any time and at any location in the world. All you need is an internet connection to link with the cloud. None of your data would be confined to a single hard drive or location. Therefore, if you want to check email anywhere in the world or if you want to upload a video to share it with your clients, you can do it within a few minutes.

These days, businesses have opted in favor of video marketing. Almost every business is into running video marketing campaigns and, for that, you need cloud services at any cost. Cloud services make it easier for you to upload a video from anywhere so your customer base can access it without any delay. Similarly, researches that are conducted these days are different than the ones that were conducted a few years back. We live in a day and age where the preferred method of doing research is ethnography. Ethnographies study consumers in a live environment. Companies prefer studying the market in real-time. With the dynamics of research changing so drastically, you can only imagine the number of video files that companies have to store these days.

This much data cannot be stored on hard drives. That's the primary reason why companies turn to cloud computing.

With cloud computing, you can store as much data as you want without having to worry about running out of space or overloading the server.

2- No Need to Spend Money on High Memory Computers

With the movement of your files to the web, you no longer have to pay for expensive high memory computers. You simply need a device that is powerful enough to run the middleware needed to connect to the cloud system. If you have ever gotten a chance to visit a company's data center, you would know how many computers there are. Companies need that kind of storage space to meet the needs and demands of their business. The more a company decides on expanding its operations, the more will be its need for storage space. That's one of the primary reasons why building a local data center is considered an expensive albeit strategic decision.

But with cloud computing, companies need not worry about increasing their expense. In fact, they don't even have to think about allocating a room, a floor, or a whole building for the purpose of running an in-house data center with hundreds of high memory computers.

3- No Software Licenses for Every Employee

In a company-wide setting, when you use the cloud, your

employer will not need to buy software or software licenses for every employee. Instead, all you have to do is pay a fee to a cloud computing company to let all their employees access a suite of software online.

As it turns out, companies, whether big or small, tend to use a number of software these days. You can't name a company that works without a variety of software today. With a growing dependence on software, you can very well imagine how high the expense would be. But cloud computing can save your company from incurring such a hefty bill. You can have as many software as you want on the cloud without having to worry about crossing your budget constraints.

Besides all that, there's another aspect that must be brought to users' attention. Cloud computing is famous for offering you the online versions of the latest software, but there's another benefit as well. You don't have to renew the licenses or upgrade software at all. All necessary upgrades are done by the cloud computing service provider. You can use the latest and upgraded version of software without a cent going out of your pocket.

The latest versions of software come out every year – for instance, MS Office. But you don't have to purchase those versions every year. You can pay for a subscription and use them online. All the new features in software are upgraded on cloud computing. The software becomes more efficient with time and benefits your business in unique ways.

4- No Physical Space Is Required at All

Servers and digital storage take up physical space, which you may have to rent. Cloud computing companies store your data on their hardware, so no physical space is required at the front end. When all the equipment that is used in cloud computing is of the cloud computing service provider, you don't have to own anything to be able to use cloud computing services. That means you don't have to arrange for any sort of physical space for any equipment.

Sometimes, companies that decide on having an in-house data center spend millions of dollars trying to get the right place of the right size for the data center. However, that's none of your concern if you're opting for cloud computing. All you have to do is enjoy the cloud services against a small amount of fee. There's absolutely no need to make room for hundreds of servers and other IT equipment that are part and parcel of a data center.

5- No Cost Related to IT Problems

Streamlining the software and hardware will reduce IT

problems and costs. When you won't be running a data center of your own, you won't need all the equipment that is required to run a data center. That means you won't have to bear the steep costs of repair and maintenance. There won't be major IT-related problems either.

With cloud computing, you don't need excessive equipment – no servers and no cooling equipment. The costs for operating a server are based on the capacity of a server. If the server becomes overloaded, it will fail to perform, meaning you would have to call for repairs immediately to get the data center up and running as soon as possible. Problems like this occur all the time. Even multinational corporations have to deal with issues like these, but for them, incurring such repair and maintenance expenses is no big deal. However, for small companies and startups, the recurring nature of these expenses can prove to be costly and troublesome.

One of the reasons why sometimes you can't access the website of a company or avail their service is because their servers are not responding. They get overloaded with all the heavy traffic and sometimes cannot be restored to normal for days. But that's not the case with cloud computing. Cloud applications are available 24 hours a day, 7 days a week, 365 days a year, without any error or delay in the service. All you need to access these applications is a consistent internet connection.

6- Taking Advantage of Combined Processing Power

The cloud computing back end is a network of computers. You may be able to take advantage of the networks' combined processing power to speed up operations. There's a reason why more and more companies these days are turning towards cloud computing, which is speed. Operations can be carried out at a speedy pace as compared to carrying out the same business operations via an in-house data center. And in today's business operations, speed is all that matters. Delays are absolutely intolerable.

7- Save a Major Chunk of Your IT-Related Costs

When it comes to saving costs, businesses tend to consider every idea presented to them. When it comes to saving costs, every idea is worth giving a try. That's the reason perhaps why every business owner these days is giving cloud computing a try, especially the ones who are starting out with their new business ventures. As it turns out, cloud computing is a perfect way to save costs and increase your revenue streams. At the end of the day, that's what matters the most in businesses – multiplying profit margins.

According to researches done on the cost-effectiveness of

cloud computing, the cloud-based solutions can save up to 95 percent of a company's IT costs. Isn't that grand? The percentage is so high because companies save a lot of money on their electricity bills. The fact of the matter is that data centers need to run 24x7, and that makes them consume a tremendous amount of power. As a result, an unavoidable spike in electricity bills is evident. Fortunately, cloud computing is a perfect solution to that problem. It reduces electricity consumption and brings the energy bills back to normal.

8- Cloud Computing Is Super Safe

Cloud companies live and die by their reputations and reliability. Therefore, these companies do everything in their power to secure your data and files. With so many security measures, it's really hard for a hacker to hack cloud computing services. There are some authentication techniques that the cloud companies use to protect your information. They allow you to use usernames and difficult passwords. They keep a security check on who's signing into your account and from where. If someone tries to sign in to your account from a new location, they shoot an automated email, warning you that someone from an unknown computer has tried to sign in. You can then verify if this is indeed you, or someone else – someone potentially dangerous.

As a matter of fact, it's really easy to create a backup while using cloud services. You can store all your files on a different cloud service so your files stay safe, just in case something happens. There are several other security practices that cloud companies use to keep your files safe. For instance, they make really good use of authorization practices.

To that end, one of the most common authorization practices that you would find on cloud services is that the user is allowed to create a list of people who are authorized to access certain information stored on the cloud system. Here's a simple example that will help you understand the practice more easily:

An employee might only be able to use certain applications stored on the cloud that are pertinent to their work, while the rest of the applications might be restricted. That's because that particular employee's name and ID must be on the list that is allowed to access the selected applications.

9- Cloud Computing Is Environmentally Friendly

This is perhaps one of the most pivotal benefits of cloud computing. Green computing is the hot topic these days. But what does it actually mean to you and your business? How could you implement it in your business processes to get the most out of it? Questions such as these often pop up in our minds when we hear of green computing.

Simply put, green computing or green IT is the practice and study of environmentally sustainable computing. With the increase in e-waste, capital expenses, and operating expenses, green computing seems to be the best alternative. Besides that, there are other reasons as to why companies need to adopt green computing. These reasons include the need for better branding, environment and climate change, increasing demand and cost of energy, and industry and government regulations.

The benefits of green computing are numerous. Green computing can help you cut costs, it will provide your business with better branding, enhanced utilization of resources, help sustain the environment, and above all, a great CSR opportunity because adopting green technology improves corporate image.

Now, the question in your mind would be how businesses should implement green computing? To reduce e-waste, save energy, and cut costs, businesses can implement green computing by adopting cloud computing. Cloud computing doesn't have any severe effects on the environment. Instead, it's a great opportunity to conserve our gradually deteriorating environment.

- Cloud computing reduces energy consumption by up to 95 percent.
- Cloud-based solutions reduce up to 90 percent of emissions.
- Cloud applications are an excellent way to reduce electronic waste in landfills.
- Cloud technology happens to be more energy efficient than any other current method.

Despite the advantages, some people are still concerned about cloud computing's negative impacts, such as:

- Cloud services are powered by electricity.
- Electricity is powered by fossil fuels.

Wouldn't that mean that carbon emissions would increase if businesses were to adopt cloud computing and shift their operations to cloud solutions? No, carbon emissions won't increase. The reason why switching to cloud services won't increase pollution is that companies, such as Apple and Facebook, are beginning to use renewable energy to power their clouds, rather than fossil fuels.

Cloud computing is an incredibly useful and efficient resource that more and more companies are starting to utilize. What's more, cloud computing is an eco-friendly server system that can help cut down on pollution, emissions, and waste.

10- Cloud Computing Is Cost-Effective

Truth be told, the infrastructure of cloud computing is very expensive. That's the reason why cloud service providers charge a fee, either monthly or annually, when you want to store more than a few gigabytes of data. But that fee is still a lot easier to afford than the monthly or annual cost of running a local data center.

You can hit your limit right in the middle of transferring a hundred or so pictures or videos. Of course, you will see an error message appear on your screen, saying that you have run out of space. However, that doesn't mean you are doomed for good. That error message will be accompanied by instructions on how you can purchase more virtual space. In addition to that, internet service providers may implement bandwidth caps, which limit the amount of data you are allowed to transfer over their network each month. When you go over the limit, providers will begin to charge you fees or slow down your connection or cut off the service altogether. Despite all that, cloud computing is much cheaper than maintaining a data centre

JAY A. COHEN

"Cloud is about how you do computing, not where you do computing."

-Paul Maritz, CEO of VMware.

Chapter 9
Web Hosting vs. Cloud Hosting

Web hosting services offer servers to multiple companies. They wouldn't have to build their own data centers. However, with cloud computing, a company can use multiple servers that are readily available. The cloud hosting can manage higher traffic and higher data security. They are more effective and efficient than a web hosting service.

Since the trends have significantly changed, modern businesses are all about cloud hosting. However, for the sake of argument, I will discuss both web hosting, which is somewhat an old method, and cloud hosting as well, which is obviously the newer method.

The purpose of this chapter is to define both, web hosting and cloud hosting so that you may understand the difference between the two ways you can host your business website and maintain your web presence. So, let's start with web hosting.

Web Hosting Explained

Understanding web hosting is important, even though business models have shifted towards cloud hosting these days. There are two reasons why you should understand what web hosting is. First, not all companies in the world have moved to the cloud. Some big companies still use web hosting services and feel comfortable with that.

Second, you need to know the difference between web hosting and cloud hosting so you may make an informed decision when the time comes for you to start your own business. As it turns out, cloud hosting is the easier option for SMEs and startups as well. Let's start with the basics. For those who don't know, hosting is the home of your website. If you want to make a business website, you will need a place to host it. Simply put, that's exactly what web hosting is. Now, as it turns out, there are different types of hosting services. You have shared hosting, reseller hosting, and virtual private servers that most of us commonly identify as VPS. Then there are dedicated servers as well. Nonetheless, in this chapter, we'll focus more on shared web hosting because that's the common, popular, and affordable type of hosting.

So what is hosting? Hosting basically is the computer and network infrastructure that makes your website available online. It also provides other key services, like email, for you. So, the question in your mind right now should be how it all works.

Well, it all starts with a server, which basically is a powerful computer. This powerful computer is stored in a highly secure, purpose-built multi-million dollar facility called the data center. Most big companies prefer to build their own data centers for many reasons that we have already discussed in the previous chapters of this book.

The data center provides the network and powered connectivity with temperature control backup systems, fire suppression systems, and of course, peak levels of physical security. When we talk about security, it is also critically needed at the server level. That's why the servers are actually built with dual components. There are four critical components in a server, including hard drives and power supply units.

The reason why servers are so robust is to make sure that your website is available at all times. Think about it. Companies, whether big or small, cannot afford to go offline for even a few seconds. There's fierce competition in the digital market and the absence of merely one minute can cost a company millions of dollars.

When you order hosting services, you are actually purchasing the physical disk space on the server as well as the bandwidth, which is a network connection for the server. You can often see hosting advertised in terms of disk space and bandwidth. For example, you might see 5 GB of disk space and 100 GB of bandwidth per month. The disk space covers your website and all your files, including key files, and important things like your emails. As for the monthly bandwidth allowance, it is the amount of traffic that comes in and out of your website and your hosting space. Most of the traffic is made up by the emails coming in and out, but also things like people visiting your website and where you actually publish your website files.

Managing Web Hosting

To manage your web hosting, you will need access to a user-friendly interface or the control panel. One of the most popular ones is called cPanel. This allows you to manage key areas of your hosting things, like setting up email addresses, managing domains, and forwarding and managing databases. This basically shields you from any technical aspects of hosting.

If you want to build your own website, you can also use tools like website builder, which allows non-technical users to build and maintain a website for their business. These website building tools use templates or pre-made templates. All you have to do is add your own text and images, then publish it. For more advanced users or if you have got a web designer, there are more tools and applications, which are included for free. You can manage databases and also use other tools to build your website. These tools and applications include popular content management systems, like WordPress, as well as more advanced e-commerce tools, like PrestaShop and Magento. With the help of these tools, you can start selling online. Other security features that you might need while hosting your own website include anti-spam software and data backup. These things ensure the integrity of your email and your data.

Transferring from One Hosting Company to Another

If you're with one hosting company and you want to transfer to another hosting company, you can do that easily. In fact, it's a straightforward method. This is a process that is commonly referred to as migration. What happens during migration is that files are copied from your current hosting to your new hosting service. There are just a couple of changes that need to be made to your domains and profile server settings for the process to be fully completed.

Choosing the Right Hosting Service

There are different types of web hosting accounts to choose from. And it can get a little confusing and a little overwhelming to keep tabs and to understand the different types of hosting and make the right decision for your firm. Guiding you on that is the purpose of this chapter. This section will help you choose the right web hosting for your business – whether you want one website, multiple websites, an e-commerce website, or online learning course website. If you want to choose the right kind of hosting service for your business, you need to use the four S's of hosting to make the right decision.

- The first S is speed. Depending on how fast you need your website to load, you need to rate a web hosting service.

- Support is the second S. This is essentially customer support service. You need to see if the hosting service provides client support if your website goes offline or is down. Not just that, support also means that hosting service will help clients if they can't log in to their WordPress account, cannot update a plugin, etc.

- The third S is security. This includes a couple of things. Number one, it includes a free SSL certificate, which is a must nowadays. There are a lot of hosts that do not provide this and there some who are getting on the bandwagon, but security goes a lot further than just that. Another side of security is to check if the hosting service is taking proactive measures to prevent and block brute-force attacks on your website, scanning for vulnerabilities on your website, and other blind spots like that.

- The last S is a specialty. This is checking whether or not a web host provides any specific features for WordPress users. Specialty is a staging area. The hosting service will create a separate instance of your website where you can go and test different things, test different designs, and update plugins – all to see if it causes any problems.

A Brief Description of Different Types of Hosting

Some web hosting types are closely related, but you can easily break them down into seven different categories.

1- Basic Shared Hosting

We have already discussed basic shared hosting in this chapter. A lot of us start with our first website on basic shared hosting. With basic shared hosting, there aren't many special features for WordPress users. Most hosts do not have special WordPress related support, so you can't ask them to reset your WordPress password. This is the most affordable type of hosting, but as we crave for a more professional or complex websites, we move on.

2- Managed WordPress Hosting – cPanel and Custom

cPanel is a control panel that allows you to install your websites. It also allows you to create email accounts to access the file system and do stuff that makes it easier for you to manage all your different websites. This is slightly expensive than the basic shared hosting, but it tends to be a more stable and smoother experience. Since this is a managed WordPress, they will have some way of updating your plugins and themes for you, as well as some additional features like staging environments.

The custom managed WordPress hosting providers have done away with industry-standard cPanel and have instead created their own custom control panel for optimal performance. Managed WordPress hosting that has its own custom panel does not include email hosting. However, you can get phenomenal speed and specialty services from this kind of host regardless.

3- Managed WooCommerce Hosting

This is a rather new and unique type of web hosting, and there are only a handful of hosts of this kind. It's a lot like managed WordPress hosting, but its environment has been optimized for woo-commerce and e-commerce shops. This web hosting service is included with some services that are outside WordPress that make running an e-commerce shop much easier, much smoother, and much more efficient and strategic. This is a newer type of hosting that you might not see being used everywhere just yet.

4- Reseller Hosting

Reseller Hosting is basically like basic shared hosting, but it allows you to create these separate containers of web hosting accounts that you can use for individual clients. You can have any type of hosting plan that allows you to host more than one website, and you can then place your client's website on it. The only thing is that you have your personal website and your client website, even if you're not going to give your client the login details because then they would be able to access your stuff. So that's what reseller hosting is for. Typically, you find this with cPanel based hosting. What it does is that it allows you to create unique individual cPanel account so you can keep your client websites and email accounts separate from each other. Furthermore, it allows you to create these cPanel accounts. You pay one fee, and you get a certain amount of resources that you can allocate to each one of your clients accordingly. This is actually great if you're a web agency and you want to keep all your clients separate.

5- Virtual Private Servers (VPS)

Virtual Private Servers make it easy for you to add email accounts, have multiple websites, and more. However, you also get some dedicated resources as well. This is the type of hosting that is slightly costly, and you can also use it most of the time if it comes with something that's called WHM. WHM allows you to create separate cPanel accounts if you want to. Now VPS services do come with support, so you can go and ask for help if you run into any trouble.

6- Dedicated Server

Some hosting companies have full dedicated servers, so the entire machine and 100 percent of its resources are for you. Although dedicated servers have more resources, those resources are dedicated to you.

7- Cloud Hosting

From here, we will move on to the next part of our chapter, which is cloud hosting. Cloud hosting has been going on for a while now. If truth be told, cloud hosting is not for the faint at heart. There's no control panel, and there's no client support available to you. What you're doing in cloud hosting is buying dedicated resources, and there's no control panel to manage it. So, in short, you're out on your own. The best thing about cloud hosting is that you can get the highest quality service at the lowest prices. Indeed, it is extraordinary what you can achieve with cloud hosting.

Explaining Cloud Hosting

Since this is the essence of this chapter, I'll start with the basics. Computers used to work alone, inside a home or a business, but thanks to the internet, we can use the power of computers at a completely different location – what we call in the cloud. I've already gone through the definition of cloud computing several times in this book. So, let's directly jump to cloud hosting. Cloud hosting is defined as, *"Services that provide hosting on virtual servers that can pull their computing resource from widespread primary networks of physical web servers."*

Generally, clients who want to benefit from cloud hosting can avail the service as much as they need to, based on their requirements at any stage. Using cloud hosting can result in cost savings. That's because clients only have to pay for what they use. Moreover, the clients can access it at any time. They don't have to pay for additional capacity.

How Cloud Hosting Works

There are two different kinds of clouds; public and private. In a public cloud, you will easily come across various examples of cloud hosting that involve the use of different public cloud models. These models include hosting on virtual servers that can pull a resource from a large and extensive pool of other virtual servers that are available publicly. The public networks are used for transmitting data; data that is physically stored on the underlying shared servers that form the cloud resource. Public clouds always include basic security measures to ensure that data is secure and kept private. This alone will be sufficient for most installations.

Private clouds are generally considered more suitable where privacy and security are of utmost importance. Private clouds mostly use ring-fenced resources, which include networks and servers that are either located onsite or with the cloud service provider.

The Features and Benefits of Cloud Hosting

Cloud hosting happens to be an alternative to hosting websites on dedicated or shared servers, commonly referred to as single servers. The following features and benefits make cloud hosting all the rage these days.

1- Reliability

Instead of hosting on a single physical server, cloud hosting allows you to use resources (like disk space) from an extensive network of underlying physical servers. Even if one of these physical servers goes offline, the user will not experience any effect on availability. That's because virtual servers can continue to pull a resource from other physical servers of the network that are online.

2- Physical Security

These underlying physical servers are located within huge data centers. Due to this, they benefit from security measures that are implemented to prevent different people, essentially hackers, from accessing or harming their online files.

3- Scalability

With cloud hosting, the resource is available in real-time and on-demand. The resource is not limited to the physical capacity or constraints of just one server. For instance, if a client's website demands extra resource from the hosting platform because of an increase in visitor traffic or the implementation of the new feature, the resource can be accessed seamlessly.

4- Utility-Based Costing

The best thing about cloud hosting is that the client only has to pay for what it has actually used. The resource is always available for an increase in demand, but the capacity is never wasted if the demand is low or remains unused.

5- Efficient Load Balancing

In cloud hosting, load balancing is done by utilizing the

software. Therefore, load balancing is scalable and responsive to changing demands.

Cloud Hosting vs. Traditional Hosting

If you are setting up a business website or a blog, you will need a hosting solution that allows you to put your website's content up on the internet. It's important to know that there are two different types of hosting solutions, namely cloud hosting and traditional hosting.

Traditional hosting has two types, dedicated and shared hosting, both of which I have already discussed in this chapter. With dedicated hosting, the client pays for all the resources of one or more servers, and the client has full control over the allocated servers, CPU, memory, and driver space. However, with shared hosting, the resources of a single server are shared by the website of different clients and each client pays for the set amount of resources of a single server, such as CPU and the driver space.

Traditional hosting, especially shared hosting, has its drawbacks because the resources of a single server are shared among different websites. Thus, a sudden spike in traffic to those websites leads to a decrease in your performance. Moreover, security breaches and performance issues with other websites can affect your website as well.

Furthermore, if the server itself has technical problems, everything stored on that server will be affected. Critical information and data can be lost. That's something companies these days cannot afford.

Generally, if the traffic of your own website is predictable, the shared hosting may be a good solution for you. However, if the traffic of your website is increasing rapidly due to a new product or feature, you may be constrained by the amount of storage that you currently have. In this case, you will have to allocate additional server space to add storage space and processing power. But if the traffic of your website falls again, you will have to pay for the resources that you are not using.

On the other hand, using cloud hosting is a better option in many respects. Cloud hosting offers a level of scalability that traditional hosting fails to provide. Cloud hosting providers provide virtual space on-demand as a virtual machine. Moreover, instead of paying for the set amount of space on a single server, you pay for what you actually use. With cloud hosting, your web application is hosted in the cluster composite of a set of servers instead of one. Additionally, the web traffic is balanced out across the server using the load balancer.

If an individual server has a technical problem or goes down, the other servers will continue to work normally without problems. Owing to this redundancy, cloud hosting is considered more elastic. Also, you don't need to pay for extra storage or processing capacity that you don't use. In addition to that, cloud hosting is more rapidly scalable than traditional hosting. If an application or website receives less traffic, the cloud providers scale up and down automatically without you having to worry about scalability issues. With cloud hosting, there is absolutely no need to manually add or remove resources as there is in shared hosting.

Keeping these differences between traditional hosting and cloud hosting in view, you can make your own decision. With these sharp differences, you can easily see that cloud hosting saves people from a lot of trouble and unwanted stress. Business operations are carried out easily and securely with cloud hosting, and the hosting services can adjust according to the needs of your business with no manual intervention.

With digital methods taking over conventional ideas, running businesses have become relatively easier. With digital methods, businesspersons get a variety of options and features that allow them to expand their business – even on a global scale. Needless to say, cloud hosting is one of those methods that create infinite ease for businesspersons, especially the ones who are starting with their business ventures and are running short on capital.

Surely cloud hosting has enabled people to launch their startups in different fields, which was sort of impossible for them before the advent of cloud computing. Thanks to cloud computing, such people are free to test their business ideas with almost no barrier holding them back.

"The cloud services companies of all sizes...The cloud is for everyone. The cloud is a democracy."

-Marc Benioff, Founder, CEO and Chairman of Salesforce

Chapter 10
Making the Cloud Work for You

The future of the world rests on the shoulders of cloud computing. Multiple companies have switched to cloud computing to smoothen their processes. For example, you might use an application on the website to track an order. The application that enables you to track the order is operated by another application on the cloud server. That's how simple cloud computing has made things for businesses.

If truth be told, cloud computing has changed, or should I say revolutionized, small businesses. If you ask established businesspersons, they will tell you directly what concerns business owners have when they think about moving to cloud computing. When they first consider cloud computing, business owners always ask where I ought to begin, or where I ought to start from. The best answer to give these people is that they should focus on how cloud computing allows them to deliver continuity and SLAs very quickly for the company. And at the same time, they are not required to pay for services that are not being used. Hence, actually having that flexibility by utilizing the cloud model gives you tons of benefits.

Let's take a brief moment and find out how the increased use of virtualization has affected the small business IT setup. If truth be told, over the past decade, virtualization technology has changed from maybe only one choice to a range of options in the market. Today, we have everything, from licensable options to choices that specifically focus on application virtualization and virtual machines as well. This gives companies an option where they should have a strategy for a multi-hypervisor environment.

Cloud computing is apparently based on virtual techniques, and it has improved IT systems for small companies. One of the interesting trends happening in the market right now is the placement of the end-user computer in the data center. This is actually reducing the number of computers that used to sit under desks for years and now, they can be repurposed into the data center.

That's what's called VDI. Now typically, this can be in a virtualized environment, but when we're talking of much higher compute graphical workloads, you have to look at the virtualized CAD workstations. Typically, this has been a one to one contention ratio to hardware to the user. Now on the latest platforms and graphical capabilities coming out from the vendors, we can do multiple users to one server. This is actually changing the market.

At this juncture, the million-dollar question if there is a bigger technology coming up in the market that could change business drastically? The answer is yes. That big thing is Big Data. You need to figure out a way to use the data that you already have rather than just archiving it off into a pool that does nothing for you. With Big Data, not only can you provide low-cost storage, but also a platform that enables you to search your data, perform analytics using your data, and provide something new to your business by creating a learning cluster.

Cloud Computing Is the Future for Business

According to Karl Deacon, the CTO for the outsourcing services at CapGemini, there's no denying the fact that cloud computing is the future. Instead of buying, acquiring, or configuring and implementing information technology to run your business processes, you can rent information technology assets from a provider by using cloud-based infrastructure. With cloud computing, we can only use the amount of resources we need and only pay for what we use. Moreover, with cloud computing, we don't have underutilized assets sitting around in our companies that we have spent money on.

Virtualization software is all about getting the assets to work harder for the money you spent on them. It's about getting your return on investment and improving that. So instead of 12, 15 or even 20% percent utilization of that server or that storage device, you'll get around 75 to 80% performance from the server's operations.

When you look at the cloud alternative as opposed to virtualizing your own servers in your own company, the cloud is the massive scale of that. Indeed, it's highly virtualized technological infrastructure that's spread all over the world, and you buy the use of small components of it. With such services, we can achieve enormous maximization of our assets at a very large scale so we can cater to multiple clients and offer unique commercial models that are attractive.

How Cloud Computing Benefits Companies

Many companies are reaping the extraordinary benefits offered by cloud services. What cloud service providers are doing these days is that they bring together different cloud services infrastructure, a variety of software applications –

for example, from the cloud – and integrate these services. Then, they provide the integrated services to the client as a service that they pay for as they use it. This way, these companies are getting a wide number of cloud services to fulfill the needs of their e-commerce environment business processes and transactions.

The speed at which cloud service providers can offer companies things like software as service capabilities, which are effectively business applications except they run in the cloud, is just terrific. Similarly, the speed at which these companies can use these services is also huge and significantly faster than what you can do by building your own IT applications and integrating them all.

With the help of cloud computing, the cost and the performance of IT in business can be scaled up and down with the business revenues. This ensures that if a business succeeds, the amount of information technology needed to deliver its business processes and transactions will also need to increase. Now, you don't have to wait for three months to go out and buy another server and bring that in and implement it. Hence, the great benefit of using cloud computing is scalability. Many cloud service providers today call that elasticity of cloud type services. You can use as much or as little as you want and you pay for what you use and no more or less.

Cloud service providers are leading the thinking and also the early deployment of cloud services. They continue to help the companies with their strategies and implementation of cloud services.

Various Reasons Why Companies Are Adopting Cloud Computing

The question in everybody's mind is why companies are adopting cloud computing so rapidly. Sure, it's a modern technology that offers companies a variety of options and diverse opportunities, but that's not it. There are reasons, in fact, strategic reasons, which make cloud computing the most sought-after technology in recent times.

The chief reason why more and more companies opt for cloud computing is that it allows for trading capital expenses with variable expenses. Additionally, company managements are always up for adopting such ideas as they are very attractive to them. Instead of having to layout all that capital for data centers and servers before you know how you're going to use them, you can pay as you consume resources on a variable basis. That of itself is very appealing. On top of trading capital expense for the variable expense, companies love the fact that in the cloud, they get to pay a lower variable expense.

According to Andy Jassy, Senior Vice President of Amazon Web Services, there's a very interesting virtuous circle going on, which is that as we have more companies that use cloud computing, it means we have to buy more infrastructure. But as we buy more infrastructure, we get economies of scale, which lowers our infrastructure cost. As we lower our infrastructure cost, we're able to lower our prices, which, in turn, drives more customers. This is a very useful virtuous circle for both customers and Amazon Web Services. Alas, the story doesn't end there.

Jassy continued saying that it turns out that you can inject energy into this flywheel. As we add new services and features and expand our global footprint, we continue to partner with our very large and growing ecosystem. More companies can run the applications they want on AWS, and more companies still can get help from system integrators to properly move to the cloud. It turns out that we're able to spin that flywheel faster as we're able to continue to innovate our infrastructure. So in our data centers and on our network and with our hardware, we're able to get better economies of scale, which lets us lower infrastructure costs as well as our prices to once again spin the wheel faster. Amazon Web Services has lowered its prices on 23 different occasions in the last few years, largely in the absence of any competitive pressure to do so. This fact is a huge inspiration for hundreds of companies.

The second reason why companies are running after cloud computing is that they don't have to guess what their capacity needs are anymore. Before a company takes on a new project, it has to guess what its capacity is going to be. Come to think of it, that's rather hard to do without knowing the customer's response. Hence, what happens is that companies make some projection, which almost never matches the actual usage of capacity.

The thing is that in the beginning, a company is sitting on a lot of wasted capital and resource until your new application takes off. Once the application takes off, you're left with limited capacity. The company needs to decide whether it should give bad customer experience, which most companies don't choose, or you have to run around like a chicken with your head cut off and find somebody who can get you that infrastructure quickly, but you almost always overpay and over commit to doing it. On the other hand, in the cloud, that problem doesn't even exist. For starters, companies don't have to guess their capacity. Companies can provide as much resource as they think they will need early on. If it turns out that the company will need more capacity, it can seamlessly scale up. And if it turns out that the company won't need as much capacity as it provisioned at one point, it can always give it back to the cloud service providers and stop paying for it. Now, that's a very different model than what has been the status quo over the last 30 years.

The third big reason why companies are shifting cloud technology is that the cloud dramatically improves how quickly they can get to market with whatever applications they are thinking about. A couple of decades back in time, if you would talk to an engineer, an enterprise, or a company, and ask them how long it takes you to provision a server for something new, the respondent would undoubtedly say 6 to 20 weeks. Come to think of it, that's completely maddening. 6 to 20 weeks for a single server is total madness. But what's worse is that it stifles innovation. People figure why to bother if it's going to take so long just to get a server. On the other hand, in the cloud, you can provision completely on your self-service hundreds and even thousands of servers in minutes without having to talk to anybody. That completely changes how you deploy applications.

There are two highly important things that you have to bear in mind. Number one is the ability to experiment. And number two, if those experiments don't work, you don't have to live with the collateral damage of a failed experiment. In the cloud, you can spin out thousands of instances in minutes. Companies can try out any experiment that it wants to carry out and if that experiment doesn't work, they can move on to something else. The fact is that companies want to change the game. More importantly, they want to move their businesses forward quickly.

The fourth reason is that companies are running out of resources. Yes, they have scarce resources. For instance, take software companies. Software engineers have this long list of priorities and projects that the company wants them to do, and they're left with this unpleasant experience of having to try to prioritize between them. As it turns out, these decisions are really hard to take. Instead of having these resources focused on the infrastructure, these companies can focus these resources on projects that move their mission or business forward, and that's a huge advantage. Fortunately, cloud computing helps you achieve that advantage.

The fifth and final reason why cloud computing has become the next big thing in the corporate world is that companies can go global within minutes. They can reach the distant corners of the world within minutes. Cloud service providers can offer high-quality end-user experiences all over the world. Given the nature of the internet in the mobile world that we live in, virtually every company now, including startups, have global end-users from day one. In the old world, people used to store their applications in one data center or a couple of data centers that were located in one region.

The idea of actually being closer to their global end-users seemed like a nice, convenient thing to have, but people didn't know how to do it. They didn't know who to rely on, and they didn't know how to contract with them because they didn't speak the language.

In some cases, it seemed like it's not going to be easy. However, thanks to cloud storage, the game radically changes. You can have your application in any region of the world. This means the companies can provide a lower latency experience for their customers, which is a much better user and customer experience.

So, to summarize the benefits of moving to the cloud, you can say that with cloud computing, companies get to change the capital expense for variable expense. They no longer have to pay a lower variable expense, and they don't have to guess capacity. Companies can progress fast, which enables and encourages innovation. They get to spend their scarce resources on projects that move the business forward, and they can go global with their application's presence in mere minutes.

The Impact of Cloud on the Business World

After all that has been discussed in this chapter, you must have assessed that the impact of cloud services on the corporate world is phenomenal. Cloud computing has changed the way we do business – if just for the simple reason that when you need to buy infrastructure, it takes a tremendous amount of time to get the infrastructure installed. But with cloud services, now you can expand your business worldwide in a hybrid environment. In less than an hour, and in some cases, in less than minutes, you can have your applications everywhere.

Biotechnology today enables businesses to be more agile. It simplifies the workflows of machines and processes from business to business and from machine to machine. More importantly, it changes the experience for our consumers and users. You might be the smartest person in the world with a fantastic idea, but unless you have the technology, skills, and the technology infrastructure to capture that digitally and share it on a large scale, then you know you can't go anywhere.

Cloud computing gives a platform to share your applications globally. What cloud does is that it is packaging technologies, packaging infrastructure, packaging middleware, and packaging applications. It means that anybody with a good idea and very little money can now rapidly build and test a new business.

Businesses that are moving to the cloud are going to have a natural advantage because this new technology makes their businesses run more effectively and it increases productivity, so they are going to have a head start regarding competing in the market today. The technical agility that cloud computing provides a business is extraordinary. The ability to spin up new systems in response to new markets, new products, and new projects is also incomparable, but the most important thing that cloud computing does is that it allows companies to be agile inside the business, reducing the time it takes from coming up with an idea to actually issuing an invoice to a paying customer.

In fact, cloud computing enables vendors to do something different. The vendors are taking traditional on-premise applications and spinning new hybrid models. They are also spinning up straight up to cloud models. Cloud computing offers the ability to do something creative and something very new. It also allows for creating new revenue streams by using different models from a licensing perspective. Yet, cloud computing also provides extremely granular control around what vendors deliver to end-users regarding customer experience.

The Future of Cloud Computing

A couple of decades ago, technology permeated government first and then slowly found its way to large enterprises and then small businesses until lastly, it trickled down to individuals. However, this new wave of technology is actually the opposite. It doesn't take as much to get started with a new idea. More and more people or organizations can take advantage of technology. Come to think of it, that's the most exciting thing about the cloud. It's really brought the barrier to computing down dramatically.

According to the Lauren States, Vice President Cloud Computing at IBM, in the beginning, a lot of our conversations were about what is the cloud, what does it do, and what does cloud computing mean to us. But now, times have changed. Now, the conversations are mostly about how people can leverage the cloud. Today, you can find more and more people talking about how they can use the cloud as a delivery model, which is more efficient. They are carrying out conversations about how they can get services out faster and how they can use the cloud with social media, mobile, and data analytics.

This period we're in now is an inflection point where we really need to use the cloud for our advantage. Lauren States said that when people come to me to talk about cloud computing, the very first thing they want to talk about is how I can save my money in my IT environment. The reason behind this common question is that they want to use the funds to drive innovation and to deliver new applications and services, instead of servicing the existing infrastructure.

This is an opportunity to change the story of IT and drive down costs. Spending 60, 70 or 80 percent of your revenue to maintain the existing systems will now be history. Yes, we can now flip the economic equation. A good example of how the cloud allows businesses to grow is in the telecommunication industry. The Telecoms now have tremendous capacity and the cloud offers them the ability to bring new services to their clients quicker, more efficiently, and with fewer costs.

Similarly, for the healthcare industry, the ability to get capacity on-demand to discover genomic patterns or to test new drugs is transformational. From the user's perspective, nobody knows exactly how the cloud does that. And that's the point. The end-user has a very simple and elegant interface to this vast IT infrastructure, and they don't even realize the complexity of it. They only realize the ease of using it.

Everywhere you go, and everywhere you look, people are using the cloud. They are using it in financial services, insurance, and health care. They are using it to read, and they are using it to find information. The things that we can do now are things that nobody ever imagined doing some 20 or 30 years ago. Imagine what we are going to be able to do shortly with the cloud?

Here's a forward-thinking thought for you that I would like to leave you with – if all the computing is somewhere else if all the storage is somewhere else, then why does anyone need a computer at home in the first place? It actually depends on your frame of what a computer is. But if we regard the iPad that everyone is using these days as a window, a terminal, into this cloud environment, then technically you don't have a computer at home because everything is coming over the cloud. If you look at the way the marketplace is changing and growing with time, maybe at some point in time, there will only be five companies or five computers from five companies coming with five different clouds. This idea is something we all might have laughed at 10 years ago, but maybe its perhaps better at predicting the future and better at thinking forward than the way we might have thought it was. It's really exciting that technology, like cloud computing, allows ideas to flourish and things to be created that are revolutionary.

Bibliography

R. Neil, Determining Total Cost of Ownership for Data Center and Network Room Infrastructure, https://www.apc.com/salestools/CMRP-5T9PQG/CMRP-5T9PQG_R4_EN.pdf

What is AWS. (n.d.). Retrieved September 18, 2019, from Amazon Web Services, Inc. website: https://aws.amazon.com/what-is-aws/

What is Infrastructure as a Service (IaaS)? - Definition from Techopedia. (n.d.). Retrieved September 18, 2019, from Techopedia.com website: https://www.techopedia.com/definition/141/infrastructure-as-a-service-iaas

Contact the Author

For more information about the author you can contact him the following ways.

Written Correspondence:
JAYCO Cloud Computing Solutions LLC
2534 Birch Ave
The Villages, Florida 32162

Email: info@jaycollc.com
Website: https://www.jaycollc.com

www.ingramcontent.com/pod-product-compliance
Lightning Source LLC
Chambersburg PA
CBHW030628220526
45463CB00004B/1446